THE
GREAT AWAKENING
VS
THE GREAT RESET

ALEXANDER DUGIN

ARKTOS
LONDON 2021

ISBN	978-1-914208-47-8 (Paperback)
	978-1-914208-48-5 (Hardback)
	978-1-914208-49-2 (Ebook)
EDITING	Constantin von Hoffmeister
COVER & LAYOUT	Tor Westman

⊕ Arktos.com ▉ fb.com/Arktos ◐ @arktosmedia ▣ arktosmedia

THE GREAT AWAKENING VS THE GREAT RESET

CONTENTS

PART 4

PART 1

THE GREAT RESET

Prince Charles's Five Points

I N 2020, at the World Economic Forum in Davos, the forum's founder, Klaus Schwab, and Charles, the Prince of Wales, proclaimed a new course for humanity, the "Great Reset".

The plan, according to the Prince of Wales, consists of five points:

1. To capture the imagination and will of humanity — change will only happen if people really want it;

2. The economic recovery must put the world on the path of sustainable employment, livelihood and growth. Longstanding incentive structures that have had perverse effects on our planetary environment and nature herself must be reinvented;

3. Systems and pathways must be redesigned to advance net zero transitions globally. Carbon pricing can provide a critical pathway to a sustainable market;

4. Science, technology and innovation need reinvigorating. Humanity is on the verge of catalytic breakthroughs that will alter our view of what it possible and profitable in the framework of a sustainable future;

5. Investment must be rebalanced. Accelerating green investments can offer job opportunities in green energy, the circular and bio-economy, eco-tourism and green public infrastructure.

The term "sustainable" is a part of the most important concept of the Club of Rome — "sustainable development". This theory is based on yet another theory — the "limits of growth", according to which the overpopulation of the planet has reached a critical point (which implies the need to reduce the birth rate).

The fact that the word "sustainable" is used in the context of the Covid-19 pandemic, which, according to some analysts, should lead to population decline, has caused a significant reaction globally.

The main points of the Great Reset are:

- Control over public consciousness on a global scale, which is at the heart of "cancel culture" — the introduction of censorship on networks controlled by the globalists (point 1);

- Transition to an ecological economy and rejection of modern industrial structures (points 2 and 5);

- Humanity's entry into the 4th economic order (to which the previous Davos meeting was devoted), i.e. the gradual replacement of the workforce by cyborgs and implementation of advanced artificial intelligence on a global scale (point 3).

The main idea of the Great Reset is the continuation of globalisation and the strengthening of globalism after a series of failures: the conservative presidency of anti-globalist Trump, the growing influence of a multipolar world — especially of China and Russia, the rise of Islamic countries like Turkey, Iran, Pakistan, Saudi Arabia and their withdrawal from the influence of the West.

At the Davos Forum, representatives of the global liberal elites declared the mobilisation of their structures in anticipation of Biden's presidency and the victory of the Democrats in the USA, something they strongly desire.

Implementation

The marker of the globalist agenda is the Jeff Smith song "Build Back Better" (Joe Biden's campaign slogan). Meaning that after a series of setbacks (such as a typhoon or Hurricane Katrina), people (meaning the globalists) build back better infrastructure than they had before.

The Great Reset begins with Biden's victory.

World leaders, heads of major corporations — Big Tech, Big Data, Big Finance, etc. — came together and mobilised to defeat their opponents — Trump, Putin, Xi Jinping, Erdogan, Ayatollah Khamenei, and others. The beginning was to snatch victory from Trump using new technologies — through "capturing imaginations" (point 1), the introduction of internet censorship, and the manipulation of the mail-in vote.

Biden's arrival in the White House means that the globalists are moving on to the next steps.

This will affect all areas of life — the globalists are going back to the point where Trump and other poles of rising multipolarity had stopped them. And this is where mind control (through censorship and manipulation of social media, total surveillance and data collection of everyone) and the introduction of new technologies play a key role.

The Covid-19 epidemic is an excuse for this. Under the guise of sanitary hygiene, the Great Reset expects to dramatically alter the structures of control of the globalist elites over the world's population.

The inauguration of Joe Biden and the decrees he has already signed (overturning virtually all of Trump's decisions) means that the plan has begun to be put into action.

In his speech on the "new" course of U.S. foreign policy, Biden voiced the main directions of globalist policy. It may seem "new", but only in part, and only in comparison with Trump's policies. On the whole, Biden simply announced a return to the previous vector:

- Putting global interests ahead of national interests;

- Strengthening the structures of World Government and its branches in the form of global supranational organisations and economic structures;

- Strengthening the NATO bloc and cooperation with all globalist forces and regimes;

- The promotion and deepening of democratic change on a global scale, which in practice means:

1. escalating relations with those countries and regimes that reject globalisation — first of all, Russia, China, Iran, Turkey, etc;

2. an increased U.S. military presence in the Middle East, Europe and Africa;

3. the spread of instability and "colour revolutions";

4. widespread use of "demonisation", "de-platforming" and network ostracism (cancel culture) against all those who hold views different from the globalist one (both abroad and in the U.S. itself).

Thus, the new White House leadership not only does not show the slightest willingness to have an equal dialogue with anyone, but only tightens its own liberal discourse, which does not tolerate any objection. Globalism is entering a totalitarian phase. This makes the possibility of new wars — including an increased risk of World War III — more than likely.

The Geopolitics of the Great Reset

The globalist Foundation for Defense of Democracies, which expresses the position of U.S. neoconservative circles, recently released a report recommending to Biden that some of Trump's positions such as:

1. increasing opposition to China,

2. increased pressure on Iran

are positive, and that Biden should continue to move along these axes in foreign policy.

The report's authors, on the other hand, condemned Trump's foreign policy actions such as:

1. working to disintegrate NATO;

2. rapprochement with "totalitarian leaders" (Chinese, DPRK, and Russian);

3. a "bad" deal with the Taliban;

4. withdrawal of U.S. troops from Syria.

Thus, the Great Reset in geopolitics will mean a combination of "democracy promotion" and "neoconservative aggressive strategy of full-scale domination", which is the main vector of "neoconservative" policy. At the same time, Biden is advised to continue and increase the confrontation with Iran and China, but the main focus should be on the fight against Russia. And this requires strengthening NATO and expanding the U.S. presence in the Middle East and Central Asia.

Like Trump, Russia, China, Iran and some other Islamic countries are seen as the main obstacles.

This is how environmental projects and technological innovations (first of all, the introduction of artificial intelligence and robotics) are combined with the rise of an aggressive military policy.

PART 2

A BRIEF HISTORY OF LIBERAL IDEOLOGY: GLOBALISM AS A CULMINATION

Nominalism

To UNDERSTAND CLEARLY what Biden's victory and Washington's "new" course for the Great Reset means on a historical scale, one must look at the entire history of liberal ideology, starting from its roots. Only then are we able to understand the seriousness of our situation. Biden's victory is not a coincidental episode, and the announcement of a globalist counterattack is not merely the agony of a failed project. It is far more serious than that. Biden and the forces behind him embody the culmination of a historical process that began in the Middle Ages, reached its maturity in modernity with the emergence of capitalist society, and which today is reaching its final stage — the theoretical one outlined from the beginning.

The roots of the liberal (=capitalist) system go back to the scholastic dispute about universals. This dispute split Catholic theologians into two camps: some recognised the existence of the common (species, genus, universalia), while others believed in only certain concrete — individual things, and interpreted their generalizing names as purely external conventional systems of classification, representing "empty sound". Those who were convinced of the existence of the general, the species, drew on the classical tradition of Plato and Aristotle. They came to be called "realists", that is, those who recognised the "reality of universalia". The most prominent representative of the "realists" was Thomas Aquinas and, in general, it was the tradition of the Dominican monks.

The proponents of the idea that only individual things and beings are real came to be called "nominalists", from the Latin *nomen*. The demand — "entities should not be multiplied without necessity" — goes back precisely to one of the chief defenders of "nominalism", the English philosopher William Occam. Even earlier, the same ideas had been defended by Roscelin of Compiègne. Although the "realists" won the first stage of the conflict and the teachings of the "nominalists" were anathematised, later the paths of Western European philosophy — especially of the New Age — were followed by Occam.

"Nominalism" laid the foundation for future liberalism, both ideologically and economically. Here humans were seen only as individuals and nothing else, and all forms of collective identity (religion, class, etc.) were to be abolished. Likewise, the thing was seen as absolute private property, as a concrete, separate thing which could easily be attributed as property to this or that individual owner.

Nominalism prevailed first of all in England, became widespread in Protestant countries and gradually became the main philosophical matrix of New Age — in religion (individual relations of man with God), in science (atomism and materialism), in politics (preconditions of bourgeois democracy), in economy (market and private property), in ethics (utilitarianism, individualism, relativism, pragmatism), etc.

Capitalism: The First Phase

Starting from nominalism, we can trace the entire path of historical liberalism, from Roscelin and Occam to Soros and Biden. For convenience, let us divide this history into three phases.

The first phase was the introduction of nominalism into the realm of religion. The collective identity of the Church, as understood by Catholicism (and even more so by Orthodoxy), was replaced by Protestants as individuals who could henceforth interpret Scripture based on their reasoning alone and rejecting any tradition. Thus many aspects of Christianity — the sacraments, miracles, angels, reward after death, the end of the world, etc. — have been reconsidered and discarded as not meeting the "rational criteria".

The church as the "mystical body of Christ" was destroyed and replaced by hobby clubs created by free consent from below. This created a large number of disputing Protestant sects. In Europe and in England itself, where nominalism had borne its most thorough fruit, the process was somewhat subdued, and the most rabid Protestants rushed to the New World and established their own society there. Later, after the struggle with London, the United States emerged.

Parallel to the destruction of the Church as a "collective identity" (something "common"), the estates began to be abolished. The social hierarchy of priests, aristocracy, and peasants was replaced by undefined "townspeople", according to the original meaning of the word "bourgeois". The bourgeoisie supplanted all other strata of European society. But the bourgeois was exactly the best "individual", a citizen without clan, tribe, or profession, but with private property. And this new class began to reconstruct all of European society.

At the same time, the supranational unity of the Papal See and the Western Roman Empire — as another expression of "collective identity" — was also abolished. In its place was established an order based on sovereign nation-states, a kind of "political individual". After the end of the Thirty Years' War, the Peace of Westphalia consolidated this order.

Thus, by the middle of the seventeenth century, a bourgeois order (that is, capitalism) had emerged in the main features in Western Europe.

The philosophy of the new order was in many ways anticipated by Thomas Hobbes and developed by John Locke, David Hume and Immanuel Kant. Adam Smith applied these principles to the economic field, giving rise to liberalism as an economic ideology. In fact, capitalism, based on the systematic implementation of nominalism, became a coherent systemic worldview. The meaning of history and progress was henceforth to "liberate the individual from all forms of collective identity" to the logical limit.

By the twentieth century, through the period of colonial conquests, Western European capitalism had become a global reality. The nominalist approach prevailed in science and culture, in politics and economics, in the very everyday thinking of the people of the West and of all humanity.

The Twentieth Century and Triumph of Globalisation: The Second Phase

In the twentieth century, capitalism faced a new challenge. This time, it was not the usual forms of collective identity — religious, class, professional, etc. — but artificial and also modern theories (like liberalism itself) that rejected individualism and opposed it with new forms of collective identity (combined conceptually).

Socialists, social democrats and communists countered liberals with class identities, calling on workers around the world to unite to overturn the power of the global bourgeoisie. This strategy proved effective, and in some major countries (though not in those industrialised and Western countries where Karl Marx, the founder of communism, had hoped), proletarian revolutions were won.

Parallel to the communists occurred, this time in Western Europe, the seizure of power by extreme nationalist forces. They acted in the name of the "nation" or a "race", again contrasting liberal individualism with something "common", some "collective being".

The new opponents of liberalism no longer belonged to the inertia of the past, as in previous stages, but represented modernist projects developed in the West itself. But they were also built on a rejection of individualism and nominalism. This was clearly understood by the theorists of liberalism (above all, by Hayek and his disciple Popper), who united "communists" and "fascists" under the common name of "enemies of the open society", and began a deadly war with them.

By tactically using Soviet Russia, capitalism initially succeeded in dealing with the fascist regimes, and this was the ideological result of World War II. The ensuing Cold War between East and West by the end of the 1980s ended in a liberal victory over the communists.

Thus, the project of liberation of the individual from all forms of collective identity and "ideological progress", as understood by liberals, went through another stage. In the 1990s, liberal theorists began to talk about the "end of history" (Franics Fukuyama) and the "unipolar moment" (Charles Krauthammer).

This was a vivid proof of the entry of capitalism into its most advanced phase — the stage of globalism. In fact, it was at this time in the U.S. that the ruling elites' strategy of globalism triumphed — outlined in the First World War by Wilson's Fourteen Points, but at the end of the Cold War united the elite of both parties — Democrats and Republicans, represented mainly by "neoconservatives".

Gender and Posthumanism: The Third Phase

After defeating its last ideological foe, the socialist camp, capitalism has come to a crucial point. Individualism, the market, the ideology of human rights, democracy and Western values had won on a global scale. It would seem that the agenda is fulfilled — no one opposes "individualism" and nominalism with anything serious or systemic anymore.

In this period, capitalism enters its third phase. On closer inspection, after defeating the external enemy, liberals have discovered two more forms of collective identity. First of all, gender. After all, gender is also something collective: either masculine or feminine. So the next step was the destruction of gender as something objective, essential, and irreplaceable.

Gender required abolition, as did all other forms of collective identity, which had been abolished even earlier. Hence gender politics, the transformation of the category of gender into something "optional" and dependent on individual choice. Here again we are dealing with the same nominalism: why double entities? A person is a person as an individual, while gender can be chosen arbitrarily, just as religion, profession, nation and way of life were chosen before.

This became the main agenda of liberal ideology in the 1990s, after the defeat of the Soviet Union. Yes, external opponents stood in the way of gender policy — those countries that still had the remnants of traditional society, the values of the family, etc., as well as conservative circles in the West itself. Combating conservatives and "homophobes", that is, defenders of the traditional view of the existence of the sexes, has become the new goal of the adherents of progressive liberalism. Many leftists have joined in, replacing gender politics and immigration protection with earlier anti-capitalist goals.

With the success of institutionalizing gender norms and the success of mass migration, which is atomizing populations in the West itself (which also fits perfectly within an ideology of human rights that operates with the individual without regard to cultural, religious, social or national aspects), it became obvious that liberals had one last step left to take — to abolish humans.

After all, the human is also a collective identity, which means that it must be overcome, abolished, destroyed. This is what the principle of nominalism demands: a "person" is just a name, devoid of any meaning, an arbitrary and therefore always disputable classification. There is only the individual — human or not, male or female, religious or atheist, it depends on his choice.

Thus, the last step left for liberals, who have traveled centuries toward their goal, is to replace humans, albeit partially, by cyborgs, artificial intelligence networks, and products of genetic engineering. The optional human logically follows optional gender.

This agenda is already foreshadowed by posthumanism, postmodernism and speculative realism in philosophy, and technologically is becoming more and more realistic by the day. Futurologists and proponents of accelerating the historical process (accelerationists) are confidently looking into the near future when artificial intelligence will become comparable in basic parameters with human beings. This moment is called the Singularity. Its arrival is predicted within ten to twenty years.

The Last Battle of the Liberals

This is the context in which Biden's engineered victory in the U.S. should be placed. This is what the Great Reset or the slogan "Build Back Better" means.

In the 2000s, the globalists faced a number of problems that were not so much ideological as "civilisational" in nature. Since the late 1990s, there have been virtually no more or less coherent ideologies in the world that can challenge liberalism, capitalism and globalism. Although to varying degrees, these principles have been accepted by all or almost all. Nevertheless, the implementation of liberalism and gender politics, as well as the abolition of nation-states in favour of a world government, has stalled on several fronts.

Liberalism was increasingly resisted by Putin's Russia, which has nuclear weapons and a historical tradition of opposition to the West, as well as a number of conservative traditions preserved in society.

China, although actively engaged in globalisation and liberal reforms, was in no hurry to apply them to the political system, maintaining the dominance of the Communist Party and refusing political liberalisation. Moreover, under Xi Jinping, national trends in Chinese politics began to grow. Beijing has cleverly used the "open world" to pursue its national and even civilisational interests. And this was not part of the globalists' plans.

Islamic countries continued their struggle against Westernisation and, despite sanctions and pressure, maintained (like Shiite Iran) their irreconcilably anti-Western and anti-liberal regimes. The policies of major Sunni states, such as Turkey and Pakistan, have become increasingly independent of the West.

In Europe, a wave of populism began to rise as indigenous European discontent with mass immigration and gender politics exploded. Europe's political elites remained completely subordinated to the globalist strategy, as seen at the Davos Forum in the reports of its theorists Schwab and Prince Charles, but societies themselves came into motion and sometimes rose in direct revolt against the authorities — as in the case of the "yellow vests" protests in France. In some places, such as Italy, Germany, or Greece, populist parties have even made their way into parliament.

Finally, in 2016, in the United States itself, Donald Trump managed to become president, subjecting the globalist ideology, practices and goals to harsh and direct criticism. And he was supported by about half of Americans.

All these anti-globalist tendencies, in the eyes of the globalists themselves, could not help but add up to an ominous picture: the history of the last centuries, with its seemingly unbroken progress of the nominalists and liberals, was called into question. This was not simply the disaster of this or that political regime. It was the threat of the end of liberalism as such.

Even the theorists of globalism themselves sensed that something was wrong. Fukuyama, for example, abandoned his "end of history" thesis and suggested that nation-states still remain under the rule of liberal elites in order to better prepare the masses for the final transformation into posthumanity, supported by rigid methods. Another globalist, Charles Krauthammer, declared that the "unipolar moment" was over and that the globalist elites had failed to take advantage of it.

This is exactly the panic and almost hysterical state in which the representatives of the globalist elite have spent the last four years. And that is why the question of Trump's removal as president of the United States was a matter of life and death for them. If Trump had kept his office, the collapse of the globalist strategy would have been irreversible.

But Biden succeeded — by hook or by crook — in ousting Trump and demonizing his supporters. This is where the Great Reset comes into play. There is really nothing new in it — it is a continuation of the main vector of Western European civilisation in the direction of progress, interpreted in the spirit of liberal ideology and nominalist philosophy. Not much remains: to free individuals from the last forms of collective identity — to complete the abolition of gender and move toward a posthumanist paradigm.

Advances in high technology, the integration of societies into social networks, tightly controlled, as it now appears, by liberal elites in an openly totalitarian manner, and the refinement of ways of tracking and influencing the masses make the achievement of the global liberal goal close at hand.

But in order to deliver that decisive blow, they must, in an accelerated mode (and no longer paying attention to how it looks), swiftly clear the way for the finalisation of history. And that means that Trump's sweep is the signal to attack all other obstacles.

So we have determined our place on the scale of history. And in doing so, we got a fuller picture of what the Great Reset is all about. It is nothing less than the beginning of the "last battle". The globalists, in their struggle for nominalism, liberalism, individual liberation and civil society, appear to themselves as "warriors of light", bringing progress, liberation from thousands of years of prejudice, new possibilities — and perhaps even physical immortality and the wonders of genetic engineering, to the masses.

All who oppose them are, in their eyes, "forces of darkness". And by this logic, the "enemies of open society" must be dealt with in their own severity. "If the enemy does not surrender, he will be destroyed". The enemy is anyone who questions liberalism, globalism, individualism, nominalism in all their manifestations. This is the new ethic of liberalism. It's nothing personal. Everyone has the right to be a liberal, but no one has the right to be anything else.

PART 3

THE SCHISM IN THE U.S.: TRUMPISM AND ITS ENEMIES

The Enemy within

IN A MORE LIMITED CONTEXT than the framework of the general history of liberalism from Ockham to Biden, the Democratic victory wrested from Trump in the battle for the White House in the winter of 2020–2021, also has enormous ideological significance. This has to do primarily with the processes unfolding within American society itself.

The fact is that after the fall of the Soviet Union and the onset of the "unipolar moment" in the 1990s, global liberalism had no external opponents. At least, it seemed so at the time in the context of the optimistic expectation of the "end of history". Although such predictions proved premature, Fukuyama did not simply wonder if the future had arrived — he was strictly following the very logic of the liberal interpretation of history, and so, with some adjustments, his analysis was generally correct.

In fact, the norms of liberal democracy — the market, elections, capitalism, the recognition of "human rights", the norms of "civil society", adopting technocratic transformations, and a desire to embrace the development and implementation of high technology — especially digital technology — were in some way established throughout humanity. If some persisted in their aversion to globalisation, this could be seen as mere inertia, as an unwillingness to be "blessed" with liberal progress.

In other words, it was not ideological opposition, but only an unfortunate nuisance. Civilisational differences were to be gradually erased. The adoption of capitalism by China, Russia, and the Islamic world would sooner or later entail processes of political democratisation, the weakening of national sovereignty, and would eventually lead to the institution of a planetary system — a world government. This was not a matter of ideological struggle, but a matter of time.

It was in this context that the globalists took further steps to advance their basic program of abolishing all residual forms of collective identity. This primarily concerned gender politics as well as the intensification of migration flows, designed to permanently erode the cultural identity of Western societies themselves, including Europe and America. Thus, globalisation dealt its main blow to its own.

In this context, an "enemy within" began to emerge in the West itself. This is all those forces that resented the destruction of sexual identity, the destruction of the remnants of cultural tradition (through migration) and the weakening of the middle class. The posthumanist horizons of the impending Singularity and the replacement of humans with artificial intelligence were also increasingly worrisome. And on the philosophical level, not all intellectuals accepted the paradoxical conclusions of postmodernity and speculative realism.

In addition, there was a clear contradiction between the Western masses, living in the context of the old norms of modernity, and the globalist elites, seeking at all costs to accelerate social, cultural and technological progress as understood in the liberal optic. Thus, a new ideological dualism began to take shape, this time within the West rather than outside it. The enemies of the "open society" now appeared within Western civilisation itself. They were those who rejected the latest liberal ends and did not accept gender politics, mass migration, or the abolition of nation-states and sovereignty.

At the same time, however, this growing resistance, generically referred to as "populism" (or "right-wing populism"), drew on the very same liberal ideology — capitalism and liberal democracy — but interpreted these "values" and "benchmarks" in the old rather than the new sense.

Freedom was conceived here as the freedom to hold any views, not just those that conformed to the norms of political correctness. Democracy was interpreted as majority rule. The freedom to change gender was to be combined with the freedom to remain faithful to family values. The willingness to accept migrants who expressed a desire and proved their ability to integrate into Western societies was strictly differentiated from the blanket acceptance of all without distinction, accompanied by continuous apologies to any newcomers for the West's colonial past.

Gradually, the globalists' "internal enemy" gained serious proportions and great influence. The old democracy challenged the new one.

Trump and the Revolt of the Deplorables

This culminated in Donald Trump's victory in 2016. Trump built his campaign on this very division of American society. The globalist candidate, Hillary Clinton, recklessly called Trump supporters — i.e., the "domestic enemy" — "deplorables", which is to say "pathetic", "regrettable". The "deplorables" responded by electing Trump.

Thus, the split within liberal democracy became a crucial political and ideological fact. Those who interpreted democracy in the "old way" (as majority rule) not only rebelled against the new interpretation (minority rule directed against the majority inclined to take a populist stand, fraught with ... well, yes, of course, "fascism" or "Stalinism"), but managed to win and bring their candidate into the White House.

Trump, for his part, declared his intention to "drain the swamp", that is, to do away with liberalism in its globalist strategy and to "make America great again". Note the word "again". Trump wanted to return to the era of nation-states, to take a series of steps against the current of history (as liberals understood it). In other words, the "good old yesterday" was opposed to the "globalist today" and the "posthumanist tomorrow".

The next four years were a real nightmare for the globalists. The globalist-controlled media accused Trump of every possible sin — including "working for the Russians" because the "Russians" also persisted in their rejection of the "brave new world", sabotaging supranational institutions — up to and including the world government — and preventing gay pride parades.

All opponents of liberal globalisation were logically grouped together, including not only Putin, Xi Jinping, some Islamic leaders, but also — imagine this! — the president of the United States of America, the number one man of the "free world". This was a disaster for the globalists. Until Trump was dumped — by means of a colour revolution, engineered riots, fraudulent ballot and vote-counting methods previously used only against other countries and regimes — they could not feel at ease.

It was only after having retaken the reins of the White House that the globalists began to come to their senses. And they went back to... the old stuff. But in their case, "old" ("build back") meant returning to the "unipolar moment" — to pre-Trump times.

Trumpism

Trump rode a wave of populism in 2016 that no other European leader has managed to do. Trump thus became a symbol of opposition to liberal globalisation. Yes, it was not an alternative ideology, but merely a desperate resistance to the latest conclusions drawn from the logic and even metaphysics of liberalism (and nominalism). Trump was not at all challenging capitalism or democracy, but only the forms they had taken in their latest stage and their gradual, consistent implementation. But even this was enough to mark a fundamental split in American society.

This is how the phenomenon of "Trumpism" took shape, in many ways exceeding the scale of Donald Trump's own personality. Trump played on the anti-globalisation protest wave. But it is clear that he was not and is not an ideological figure. And yet, it was around him that the opposition bloc began to form. The American conservative Ann Coulter, the author of the book *In Trump We Trust*, has since reformulated her credo to "in Trumpism we trust".

Not so much Trump himself, but rather his line of opposition to the globalists, has become the core of Trumpism. In his role as president, Trump was not always at the height of his own articulated task. And he was not able to accomplish anything even close to "draining the swamp" and defeating globalism. But in spite of this, he became a centre of attraction for all those who were aware of or simply sensed the danger emanating from the globalist elites and the representatives of Big Finance and Big Tech inseparable from them.

Thus, the core of Trumpism began to take shape. The American conservative intellectual Steve Bannon played an important role in this process, mobilizing broad segments of young people and disparate conservative movements in support of Trump. Bannon himself was inspired by serious anti-modernist authors such as Julius Evola, and his opposition to globalism and liberalism therefore had deeper roots.

An important role in Trumpism was played by consistent paleo-conservatives — isolationists and nationalists — in the likes of Buchanan, Ron Paul, as well as adherents of anti-liberal and anti-modernist (therefore, fundamentally anti-globalist) philosophy, such as Richard Weaver and Russell Kirk, who had been marginalised by the neocons (the globalists from the right) since the 1980s.

The driving force of the mass mobilisation of "Trumpists" came to be the networked organisation QAnon, which couched its criticism of liberalism, Democrats and globalists in the form of conspiracy theories. They spread a torrent of accusations and denunciations of globalists as involved in sex scandals, pedophilia, corruption and satanism.

True intuitions about the sinister nature of liberal ideology — made evident in the latest stages of its triumphant spread over humanity — were formulated by QAnon supporters at the level of the average American and mass consciousness, which are hardly inclined towards in-depth philosophical and ideological analysis. In parallel, QAnon expanded its influence, but at the same time gave anti-liberal criticism grotesque traits.

It was the QAnon supporters, as the vanguard of mass conspiracy populism, who led the protests on January 6, when Trump supporters stormed the Capitol outraged by the stolen election. They did not achieve any goal, but only gave Biden and the Democrats an excuse to further demonise Trumpism and all opponents of globalism, equating any conservative with "extremism". A wave of arrests followed, and the most consistent "New Democrats" suggested that all social rights — including the ability to buy plane tickets — should be taken away from Trump supporters.

Since social media is regularly monitored by supporters of the liberal elite, gathering information about almost all U.S. citizens and their political preferences posed no problem. So Biden's arrival in the White House means that liberalism has taken on frankly totalitarian features.

From now on, Trumpism, populism, the defence of family values, and any hint of conservatism or disagreement with the tenets of globalist liberalism in the U.S. will be nearly equivalent to a crime — to hate speech and "fascism".

Still, Trumpism did not disappear with Biden's victory. In one way or another, it still has those who cast their votes for Donald Trump in the last election — and that is more than 70,000,000 voters.

So it is clear that Trumpism will by no means end with Trump. Half of the U.S. population has actually found itself in a position of radical opposition, and the most consistent Trumpists represent the core of the anti-globalisation underground within the citadel of globalism itself.

Something similar is happening in European countries, where populist movements and parties are increasingly aware that they are dissidents deprived of all rights and subject to ideological persecution under an apparent globalist dictatorship.

No matter how much the globalists who have retaken power in the U.S. want to present the previous four years as an "unfortunate misunderstanding" and declare their victory as the final "return to normality", the objective picture is far from the soothing spells of the globalist upper class. Not only countries with a different civilisational identity are mobilizing against it and against its ideology, but this time also half of its own population, gradually coming to realise the seriousness of its situation and beginning to search for an ideological alternative.

These are the conditions under which Biden has come to head the United States. American soil itself is burning under the feet of the globalists. And this gives the situation of "the final battle" a special, additional dimension. This is not the West against the East, not the U.S. and NATO against everyone else, but liberals against humanity — including that segment of humanity which finds itself on the territory of the West itself, but which is turning more and more away from its own globalist elites. This is what defines the starting conditions of this battle.

Individuum and Dividuum

One more essential point needs to be made clear. We have seen that the entire history of liberalism is the successive liberation of the individual from all forms of collective identity. The final accord in the process of this logically perfect implementation of nominalism will be the transition to posthumanism and the probable replacement of humanity with another — this time posthuman — machine civilisation. This is what consistent individualism, taken as something absolute, leads to.

But here liberal philosophy arrives at a fundamental paradox. The liberation of the individual from his human identity, for which gender politics prepares him by consciously and purposefully transforming the human being into a perverted monster, cannot guarantee that this new — progressive! — being will remain an individual.

Moreover, the development of networked computer technologies, genetic engineering, and object-oriented ontology itself, which represents the culmination of postmodernism, clearly point to the fact that the "new being" will not be so much an "animal" as a "machine". It is with this in mind that the horizons of "immortality" are likely to be offered in the form of the artificial preservation of personal memories (which are quite easy to simulate).

Thus, the individual of the future, as the fulfillment of the whole program of liberalism, will not be able to guarantee precisely that which has been the main goal of liberal progress — that is, their individuality. The liberal being of the future, even in theory, is not an individuum, something "indivisible", but rather a "dividuum", i.e. something divisible and made up of replaceable parts. Such is the machine — it is composed of a combination of parts.

In theoretical physics, there has long been a transition from the theory of "atoms" (i.e. "indivisible units of matter") to the theory of particles, which are thought of not as "parts of something whole" but as "parts without a whole". The individual as a whole also decomposes into component parts, which can be reassembled, but can also not be assembled, but instead used as a bioconstructor. Hence the figures of mutants, chimeras and monsters that abound in modern fiction, populating the most imagined (and therefore, in a sense, anticipated and even planned) versions of the future.

The postmodernists and speculative realists have already prepared the ground for this by proposing to replace the human body as something whole with the idea of a "parliament of organs" (B. Latour). In this way, the individual — even as a biological unit — would become something else, mutating precisely the moment it reaches its absolute embodiment.

Human progress in the liberal interpretation inevitably ends with the abolition of humanity.

This is what all those taking up the fight against globalism and liberalism suspect, albeit very vaguely. Although QAnon and their anti-liberal conspiracy theories only distort reality by lending suspect, grotesque traits, which liberals can easily refute, reality, when described soberly and objectively, is far more frightening than its most alarming and monstrous premonitions.

The Great Reset is indeed a plan for the elimination of humanity. For this is precisely the conclusion that the line of liberally understood "progress" logically leads to: striving to free the individual from all forms of collective identity cannot fail to result in the freeing of the individual from himself.

PART 4

THE GREAT AWAKENING

The Great Awakening: A Scream in the Night

WE ARE NEARING A THESIS that represents the direct opposite of the Great Reset: the thesis of the "Great Awakening".

This slogan was first put forth by American anti-globalists, such as the host of the alternative TV channel InfoWars, Alex Jones, who was subjected to globalist censorship and de-platforming from social networks in the first phase of the Trump presidency, and QAnon activists. It is important that this is happening in the U.S., where bitterness has raged between the globalist elites and the populists who had their own president, albeit for only four years and stiffened by administrative obstacles and the limitations of their own ideological horizons.

Unencumbered by serious ideological and philosophical baggage, anti-globalists have been able to grasp the essence of the most important processes unfolding in the modern world. Globalism, liberalism and the Great Reset, as expressions of the determination of liberal elites to see their plans through to the end, by any means — including outright dictatorship, large-scale repression and campaigns of total disinformation — have encountered growing and increasingly conscious resistance.

Alex Jones ends his programs with the same rallying cry — "You are the resistance!" In this case, Alex Jones himself or the activists of QAnon do not have strictly defined worldviews. In this sense, they are representatives of the masses, the same "deplorables" who were so painfully humiliated by Hillary Clinton. What is now awakening is not a camp of ideological opponents of liberalism, the enemies of capitalism, or ideological opponents of democracy. They are not even conservatives. They are just people — people as such, the most ordinary and simple. But... people who want to be and remain human, to have and keep their freedom, gender, culture, and living, concrete ties to their homeland, to the world around them, to the people.

The Great Awakening is not about elites and intellectuals, but about the people, about the masses, about people as such. And the awakening in question is not about ideological analysis. It is a spontaneous reaction of the masses, hardly competent in philosophy, who have suddenly realised, like cattle before the slaughterhouse, that their fate has already been decided by their rulers and that there is no more room for people in the future.

The Great Awakening is spontaneous, largely unconscious, intuitive and blind. It is by no means an outlet for awareness, for conclusion, for deep historical analysis. As we have seen in the Capitol footage, the Trumpist activists and QAnon participants look like characters from comic books or Marvel superheroes. Conspiracy is an infantile disease of anti-globalisation. But, on the other hand, it is the beginning of a fundamental historical process. This is how the pole of opposition to the very course of history in its liberal sense is emerging.

This is why the thesis of the Great Awakening should not be hastily loaded with ideological details, whether fundamental conservatism (including religious conservatism), traditionalism, the Marxist critique of capital, or anarchist protesting for protesting's sake. The Great Awakening is something more organic, more spontaneous and at the same time tectonic. This is how humanity is suddenly being illuminated by the consciousness of the nearness of its imminent end.

And that is why the Great Awakening is so serious. And that is why it is coming from within the United States, that civilisation where the twilight of liberalism is thickest. It is a cry from the centre of hell itself, from that zone where the black future has already partly arrived.

The Great Awakening is the spontaneous response of the human masses to the Great Reset. Of course, one can be skeptical. The liberal elites, especially today, control all major civilisational processes. They control the world's finances and can do anything with them, from unlimited issuing to any manipulation of financial instruments and structures. In their hands is the entire U.S. military machine and the management of NATO allies. Biden promises to reinforce Washington's influence in this structure, which has almost disintegrated in recent years.

Almost all of the giants of High Tech are subordinate to the liberals — computers, iPhones, servers, phones and social networks are strictly controlled by a few monopolists who are members of the globalist club. This means that Big Data, that is, the entire body of information about virtually the entire population of the earth, has an owner and master.

Technology, science centres, global education, culture, media, medicine and social services are completely in their hands.

The liberals in governments and power circles are the organic components of these planetary networks which all have the same headquarters.

The intelligence services of Western countries and their agents in other regimes work for the globalists, whether recruited or bribed, forced to cooperate or as volunteers.

One wonders: how in this situation can the supporters of the Great Awakening revolt against globalism? How — without having any resources — can they effectively confront the global elite? What weapons to use? What strategy to follow? And, furthermore, on which ideology to rely? — because liberals and globalists around the world are united and have a common idea, a common goal and a common line, while their opponents are disparate not only in different societies, but also within one and the same.

Of course, these contradictions in the ranks of the opposition are further exacerbated by the ruling elites, who are used to dividing in order to dominate. Muslims are pitted against Christians, leftists against rightists, Europeans against Russians or Chinese, etc.

But the Great Awakening is happening not because of, but in spite of all this. Humanity itself, man as *eidos*, man as a species, man as a collective identity, and in all its forms at once, organic and artificial, historical and innovative, Eastern and Western, is rebelling against the liberals.

The Great Awakening is just the beginning. It has not even begun yet. But the fact that it has a name, and that this name has appeared in the very epicentre of ideological and historical transformations, in the United States, against the background of Trump's dramatic defeat, the desperate takeover of the Capitol, and the rising wave of liberal repression, as the globalists no longer hide the totalitarian nature of both their theory and their practice, is of great (maybe crucial) importance.

The Great Awakening against the Great Reset is humanity's revolt against the ruling liberal elites. Moreover, it is the rebellion of man against his age-old enemy, the enemy of the human race itself.

If there are those who proclaim the Great Awakening, as naive as their formulas may seem, this already means that not all is lost, that a kernel of resistance is maturing in the masses, that they are beginning to mobilise. From this moment on begins the history of a worldwide revolt, a revolt against the Great Reset and its followers.

The Great Awakening is a flash of consciousness at the threshold of the Singularity. It is the last opportunity to make an alternative decision about the content and direction of the future. The complete replacement of human beings with new entities, new divinities, cannot simply be imposed by force from above. The elites must seduce humanity, obtain from it — albeit vaguely — some consent. The Great Awakening calls for a decisive "No"!

This is not yet the end of the war, not even the war itself. Moreover, it has not yet begun. But it is the possibility of such a beginning. A new beginning in the history of man.

Of course, the Great Awakening is completely unprepared.

As we have seen, in the U.S. itself, the opponents of liberalism, both Trump and the Trumpists, are ready to reject the last stage of liberal democracy, but they do not even think of a full-fledged critique of capitalism. They defend yesterday and today against a looming, ominous tomorrow. But they lack a full-fledged ideological horizon. They are trying to save the previous stage of the very same liberal democracy, the very same capitalism, from its late and more advanced stages. And this in itself contains a contradiction.

The contemporary Left also has limits in its critique of capitalism, both because it shares a materialist understanding of history (Marx agreed on the need for world capitalism, which he hoped would then be overcome by the world proletariat) and because the socialist and communist movements have recently been taken over by liberals and reoriented from waging class war against capitalism to protecting migrants, sexual minorities and fighting imaginary "fascists".

The Right, on the other hand, is confined to its nation-states and cultures, not seeing that the peoples of other civilisations are in the same desperate situation. The bourgeois nations that emerged at the dawn of the modern age represent a vestige of bourgeois civilisation. This civilisation today is destroying and abolishing what it itself created just yesterday, in the meanwhile using all the limitations of national identity to keep humanity, in a fragmented and conflicted state, from confronting the globalists.

Therefore, there is the Great Awakening, but it does not yet have an ideological basis. If it is truly historical, and not an ephemeral and purely peripheral phenomenon, then it simply needs a foundation — one that goes beyond the existing political ideologies that emerged in modern times in the West itself. Turning to any of them would automatically mean that we find ourselves in the ideological captivity of the formation of capital.

So, in seeking a platform for the Great Awakening that has erupted in the United States, we must look beyond American society and the rather short American history and look to other civilisations, above all to the non-liberal ideologies of Europe itself, for inspiration. But even this is not enough, because along with the deconstruction of liberalism, we must find support in the different civilisations of humanity, which are far from exhausted by the West where the main threat comes from and where — in Davos, in Switzerland! — the Great Reset was proclaimed.

The *Internationale* of Nations vs. the *Internationale* of the Elites

The Great Reset wants to make the world unipolar again in order to move towards a globalist non-polarity, where the elites will become fully international and their residence will be dispersed throughout the entire space of the planet. This is why globalism brings about the end of the U.S. as a country, a state, a society. This is what the Trumpists and supporters of the Great Awakening sense, sometimes intuitively. Biden is a sentence imposed on the United States, and through the U.S. on everyone else.

Accordingly, for the salvation of people, peoples, and societies, the Great Awakening must begin with multipolarity. This is not just the salvation of the West itself, and not even the salvation of everyone else from the West, but the salvation of humanity, both Western and non-Western, from the totalitarian dictatorship of the liberal capitalist elites. And this cannot be done by the people of the West or the people of the East alone. Here it is necessary to act together. The

Great Awakening necessitates an internationalisation of the peoples' struggle against the internationalisation of the elites.

Multipolarity becomes the most important reference point and the key to the strategy of the Great Awakening. Only by appealing to all nations, cultures and civilisations of humanity are we able to gather enough forces to effectively oppose the Great Reset and the orientation toward the Singularity.

But in this case the whole picture of the inevitable final confrontation turns out to be far less desperate. If we take a look at all that could become the poles of the Great Awakening, the situation presents itself in a somewhat different light. The *Internationale* of Peoples, once we begin to think in these categories, turns out to be neither a utopia nor an abstraction. Moreover, we can easily see enormous potential already and how such can be harnessed in the struggle against the Great Reset.

Let us briefly list the reserves on which the Great Awakening can count on a global scale.

The U.S. Civil War: The Choice of Our Camp

In the U.S., we have a foothold in Trumpism. Although Trump himself lost, this does not mean that he himself has washed his hands, resigned to a stolen victory, and that his supporters — 70,000,000 Americans — have settled down and taken liberal dictatorship as a given. They have not. From now on, there is a powerful anti-globalist underground in the U.S. itself, large in number (half the population!), embittered, and driven to despise liberal totalitarianism. The dystopia of Orwell's *1984* was not embodied in a communist or fascist regime, but is now in a liberal one. But the experience of both Soviet communism and even Nazi Germany show that resistance is always possible.

Today, the U.S. is essentially in a state of civil war. The liberal-Bolsheviks have seized power, and their opponents have been thrown into opposition and are on the verge of going illegal. An opposition of 70,000,000 people is serious. Of course, they are scattered and may be in disarray by the punitive raids of the Democrats and the new totalitarian technology of Big Tech.

But it is too early to write off the American people. Clearly, they still have some margin of strength, and half of the U.S. population is ready to defend their individual freedom at any cost. And today the question is exactly this: Biden or freedom? Of course, liberals will try to abolish the Second Amendment and disarm the population, which is becoming less and less loyal to the globalist elite. It is likely that the Democrats will try to kill the two-party system itself by introducing an essentially one-party regime, quite in the spirit of the current state of their ideology. This is liberal-Bolshevism.

But civil wars never have foregone conclusions. History is open, and victory for either side is always possible. Especially if humanity realises how important the American opposition is to the universal victory over globalism. No matter how we feel about the U.S., about Trump and the Trumpists, we all simply must support the American pole of the Great Awakening. Saving America from the globalists, and thus helping to make it great again, is our common task.

European Populism: Overcoming Right and Left

The wave of anti-liberal populism is not subsiding in Europe either. Although the globalist Macron has managed to contain the violent protests of the "yellow vests" and the Italian and German liberals have isolated and blocked right-wing parties and their leaders from coming to power, these processes are unstoppable. Populism expresses the same Great Awakening, but only on European soil and with European specificity.

For this pole of resistance, a new ideological reflection is extremely important. European societies are much more ideologically active than Americans, and thus the traditions of right-wing and left-wing politics — and their inherent contradictions — are much more keenly felt.

It is precisely these contradictions that the liberal elites are taking advantage of in order to maintain their position in the European Union.

The fact is that hatred for liberals in Europe is growing simultaneously from two sides: the Left sees them as representatives of big capital, exploiters who have lost all decency, and the Right sees them as provocateurs of artificial mass migration, destroyers of the last vestiges of traditional values, destroyers of European culture and the gravediggers of the middle class. At the same time, for the most part, both right-wing and left-wing populists have put aside traditional ideologies that no longer meet historical needs, and express their views in new forms, sometimes contradictory and fragmentary.

The rejection of the ideologies of orthodox communism and nationalism is generally positive; it gives the populists a new, much broader base. But it is also their weakness.

However, the most fatal thing about European populism is not so much its de-ideologisation as the persistence of the deep, mutual rejection between left and right that has persisted since previous historical eras.

The emergence of a European pole of the Great Awakening must involve the resolution of these two ideological tasks: the final overcoming of the boundary between the Left and the Right (that is, the obligatory rejection of contrived "anti-fascism" by some and of contrived "anti-communism" by others) and the elevation of populism as such — integral populism — into an independent ideological model. Its meaning and its message should be a radical critique of liberalism and its highest stage, globalism, at the same time combining the demand for social justice and the preservation of traditional cultural identity.

In this case, European populism will, first and foremost, acquire a critical mass that is fatally lacking as right-wing and left-wing populists waste time and effort on settling scores with each other, and, secondly, it will become a most important pole of the Great Awakening.

China and Its Collective Identity

The opponents of the Great Reset have another significant argument: contemporary China. Yes, China has taken advantage of the opportunities offered by globalisation to strengthen the economy of its society. But China has not accepted the very spirit of globalism, the liberalism, individualism and nominalism of globalist ideology. China has taken from the West only what has made it stronger, but rejected what would make it weaker. This is a dangerous game, but so far China has successfully coped with this.

In fact, China is a traditional society with thousands of years of history and a stable identity. And it clearly intends to remain such in the future. This is particularly clear in the policies of China's current leader, Xi Jinping. He is ready to make tactical compromises with the West, but he is strict about ensuring that China's sovereignty and independence only grow and strengthen.

That the globalists and Biden would act in solidarity with China is a myth. Yes, Trump relied on it and Bannon said so, but this is the result of a narrow geopolitical horizon and a profound misunderstanding of the essence of Chinese civilisation. China will follow its line and strengthen multipolar structures. In fact, China is the most important pole of the Great Awakening, a point which will become clear if we take as a starting point the need for an internationalisation of peoples. China is a people with a distinct collective identity. Chinese individualism does not exist at all, and if it does, it is a cultural anomaly. Chinese civilisation is the triumph of clan, folk, order and structure over all individuality.

Of course, the Great Awakening must not become Chinese. It should not be uniform at all — for every nation, every culture, every civilisation has its own spirit and its own *eidos*. Humanity is diverse. And its unity can be felt most keenly only when it is confronted with a serious threat that looms over them all. And this is precisely what the Great Reset is.

Islam against Globalisation

Another argument of the Great Awakening lies with the peoples of Islamic civilisation. That liberal globalism and Western hegemony are radically rejected by Islamic culture and the very Islamic religion on which that culture is based is obvious. Of course, during the colonial period and under the power and economic influence of the West, some Islamic states found themselves in the orbit of capitalism, but in virtually all Islamic countries there is a sustained and profound rejection of liberalism and especially of modern globalist liberalism.

This manifests itself both in extreme forms — Islamic fundamentalism — and in moderate ones. In some cases, individual religious or political movements become carriers of the anti-liberal initiative, while in other cases the state itself takes on this mission. In any case, Islamic societies are ideologically prepared for systemic and active opposition to liberal globalisation. The Great Reset's projects do not contain anything, even theoretically, that might appeal to Muslims. That is why the entire Islamic world as a whole represents one huge pole of the Great Awakening.

Among the Islamic countries, Shia Iran and Sunni Turkey are the most in opposition to the globalist strategy. Moreover, if Iran's main motivation is the religious idea of the approaching end of the world and the last battle, where the main enemy — *Dajjal* — is clearly recognised as the West, liberalism and globalism, then Turkey is driven more by pragmatic considerations, by the desire to strengthen and preserve its national sovereignty and ensure Turkish influence in the Middle East and the Eastern Mediterranean.

Erdogan's policy of gradually moving away from NATO combines the national tradition of Kemal Atatürk with a desire to play the role of the leader of Sunni Muslims, but both are achievable only in opposition to liberal globalisation, which envisions the complete secularisation of societies. the weakening (and, in the end, the abolition) of nation-states, and in the interim grants political autonomy to minority ethnic groups, a move which would be devastating for Turkey due to the large and quite active Kurdish factor.

Sunni Pakistan, which represents another form of combining national and Islamic politics, is gradually drifting further and further away from the United States and the West.

Although the Gulf countries are more dependent on the West, a closer look at Arabian Islam, and even more so Egypt, which is another important and independent state in the Islamic world, reveals social systems that have nothing to do with the globalist agenda and are naturally predisposed to side with the Great Awakening.

This is hindered only by the contradictions between Muslims themselves, skillfully aggravated by the West and globalist control centres, not only between Shia and Sunni but also regional conflicts between individual Sunni states themselves.

The context of the Great Awakening could become an ideological platform for the unification of the Islamic world as a whole as well, since opposition to the Great Reset is an unconditional imperative for almost every Islamic country. This is what makes it possible to take the globalists' strategy and opposition to it as the common denominator. Awareness of the scale of the Great Awakening would allow, within certain limits, to cancel out the acuteness of local contradictions so as to contribute to the formation of another pole of global resistance.

Russia's Mission: To Be at the Forefront of the Great Awakening

Finally, the most important pole of the Great Awakening is intended for Russia. Despite the fact that Russia has been partly involved in Western civilisation, through the Enlightenment culture during the Tsarist period, under the Bolsheviks, and especially after 1991, at every stage — in antiquity as well as in the present — the deep identity of Russian society is deeply distrustful of the West, especially of liberalism and globalisation. Nominalism is deeply alien to the Russian people in its very foundations.

Russian identity has always prioritised the common — the clan, folk, church, tradition, nation, and power, and even communism represented — albeit artificial, in class terms — a collective identity opposed to bourgeois individualism. Russians stubbornly rejected and continue to reject nominalism in all its forms. And this is a common platform for both the monarchist and Soviet periods.

After the failed attempt to integrate into the global community in the 1990s, thanks to the failure of liberal reforms, Russian society became even more convinced of the extent to which globalism and individualistic attitudes and principles are alien to Russians. This is what determines the general support for Putin's conservative and sovereign course. Russians reject the Great Reset both from the Right and from the Left — and this, together with historical traditions, collective identity, and the perception of sovereignty and state freedom as the highest value, is not a momentary, but a long-term, fundamental feature of Russian civilisation.

The rejection of liberalism and globalisation has become particularly acute in recent years, as liberalism itself has revealed its deeply repulsive features to Russian consciousness. This justified a certain sympathy among Russians for Trump and a parallel deep disgust for his liberal opponents.

On Biden's side, the attitude to Russia is quite symmetrical. He and the globalist elites in general view Russia as the main civilisational opponent, stubbornly refusing to accept the vector of liberal progressivism and fiercely defending its political sovereignty and its identity.

Of course, even today's Russia does not have a complete and coherent ideology that could pose a serious challenge to the Great Reset. In addition, the liberal elites entrenched at the top of society are still strong and influential in Russia, and liberal ideas, theories and methods still dominate the economy, education, culture and science. All of this weakens Russia's potential, disorients society, and sets the stage for growing internal contradictions. But, on the whole, Russia is the most important — if not the main! — pole of the Great Awakening.

This is exactly what all of Russian history has led up to, expressing an inner conviction that Russians are facing something great and decisive in the dramatic situation of the End Times, the end of history. But it is precisely this end, in its worst version, that the Great Reset project implies. The victory of globalism, nominalism and the coming of the Singularity would mean the failure of the Russian historical mission, not only in the future but also in the past. After all, the meaning of Russian history has been directed precisely towards the future, and the past was only preparation for it.

And in this future, which is now approaching, the role of Russia is not only to take an active part in the Great Awakening, but also to stand in the forefront of it, proclaiming the imperative of the *Internationale* of Peoples in the fight against liberalism, the plague of the twenty-first century.

Russia Awakening: An Imperial Renaissance

What does it mean for Russia in such circumstances to "awaken"? It means fully restoring Russia's historical, geopolitical, and civilisational scale, becoming a pole of the new multipolar world.

Russia has never been "just a country", much less "just one among other European countries". For all the unity of our roots with Europe, which go back to Greco-Roman culture, Russia at all stages of its history has followed its own particular path. This also had an impact on our firm and unwavering choice of Orthodoxy and Byzantinism in general, which largely determined our estrangement from Western Europe, which chose Catholicism and later Protestantism. In the modern age, this same factor of profound distrust of the West was reflected in the fact that we were not so affected by the very spirit of modernism in nominalism, individualism, and liberalism. And even when we borrowed some doctrines and ideologies from the West, they were often critical, i.e. they contained in themselves the rejection of the main — liberal-capitalistic — way of development of Western European civilisation, which was so close to us.

Russia's identity was also greatly influenced by the Eastern — Turanian — vector. As the Eurasianist philosophers, including the great Russian historian Lev Gumilev, have shown, the Mongol statehood of Genghis Khan was an important lesson for Russia in centralised organisation of the imperial type, which largely predetermined our rise as a Great Power in the fifteenth century, when the Golden Horde collapsed and Muscovite Russia took its place in the space of north-east Eurasia. This continuity with the geopolitics of the Horde naturally led to the powerful expansion of subsequent eras. At every turn, Russia has defended and asserted not only its interests, but also its values.

Thus, Russia has turned out to be the heir to two empires that collapsed at approximately the same time, in the fifteenth century: the Byzantine and the Mongol empires. Empire became our fate. Even in the twentieth century, with all the radicalism of the Bolshevik reforms, Russia remained an empire against all odds, this time in the guise of the Soviet empire.

This means that our revival is inconceivable without returning to the imperial mission laid down in our historical destiny.

This mission is diametrically opposed to the globalist project of the Great Reset. And it would be natural to expect that in their decisive rush the globalists will do everything in their power to prevent an imperial renaissance in Russia. Accordingly, we need exactly that: an imperial renaissance. Not to impose our Russian and Orthodox truth on the other peoples, cultures and civilisations, but to revive, fortify and defend our identity and to help others in their own renaissance, to fortify and defend their own, as much as we can. Russia is not the only target of the Great Reset, although in many ways our country is the main obstacle to the execution of their plans. But this is our mission — to be the *katechon*, "the one who withholds", preventing the arrival of the last evil in the world.

However, in the eyes of the globalists, other traditional civilisations, cultures and societies are also to be subject to dismantling, reformatting and transformation into an undifferentiated global cosmopolitan mass, and in the near future to be replaced by new — posthuman — forms of life, organisms, mechanisms, or their hybrids. Therefore, the imperial awakening of Russia is called upon to be a signal for a universal uprising of peoples and cultures against the liberal globalist elites. Through rebirth as an empire, as an Orthodox empire, Russia will set an example for other empires — the Chinese, Turkish, Persian, Arab, Indian, as well as the Latin American, African... and the European. Instead of the dominance of one single globalist "empire" of the Great Reset, the Russian awakening should be the beginning of an era of many empires, reflecting and embodying the richness of human cultures, traditions, religions, and value systems.

Towards the Victory of the Great Awakening

If we add together U.S. Trumpism, European populism (both right and left), China, the Islamic world and Russia, and foresee that at some point the great Indian civilisation, Latin America, and Africa, which is entering another round of decolonisation, and all the peoples and cultures of humanity in general may also join this camp, we have not mere scattered and confused marginals trying to object to the powerful liberal elites leading humanity to the final slaughter, but a full-fledged front including actors of various scales, from great powers with planetary economies and nuclear weapons to influential and numerous political, religious and social forces and movements.

The power of the globalists, after all, is based on insinuations and "black miracles". They rule not on the basis of real power, but on illusions, simulacra, and artificial images, which they maniacally try to instill in the minds of mankind.

After all, the Great Reset was proclaimed by a handful of degenerate and panting old globalist men on the verge of dementia (like Biden himself, the shriveled villain Soros, or the fat burgher Schwab) and a marginal, perverted rabble selected to illustrate the lightning-quick career opportunities for all nonentities. Of course, they have the stock exchanges and the printing presses, the Wall Street crooks and the Silicon Valley inventor junkies working for them. Disciplined intelligence operatives and obedient army generals are subordinate to them. But this is negligible compared to all of humanity, to the people of labor and thought, to the depths of religious institutions and the fundamental richness of cultures.

The Great Awakening means that we have figured out the essence of that fatal, both murderous and suicidal strategy of "progress" as the globalist liberal elites understand it. And if we understand it, then we are capable of explaining it to others. The awakened can and must awaken everyone else. And if we succeed in this, not only will the Great Reset fail, but a just judgment will be passed upon those who have made it their goal to destroy humanity, first in spirit and now in body.

APPENDIXES

About the Great Reset

(Interview in the German magazine *Deutsche Stimme*, 2 January 2021 — conducted by Alexander Markovics, and published partly in print and partly online: https://deutsche-stimme.de/alexander-dugin-nach-dem-tod-gottes-folgt-logisch-erweise-der-tod-des-menschen/)

DEUTSCHE STIMME: *Dear Professor Dugin. The global elite is discussing a strategy called "The Great Reset", which calls for a reset of capitalism and the post-liberal system after its failure during the Corona crisis. For this purpose, capitalism shall be made more sustainable in order to keep the Open Society alive, but also more repressive, in order to gain even more control over everyday life, and install a system of mass surveillance. What do you think about this new project, which is intended to save globalism?*

ALEXANDER DUGIN: I think that this is precisely not a new strategy, but a new term of the globalists. In the history of globalisation, the term reset is a very interesting concept. The content is the same as was the New World Order, globalisation, One World, End of History, the promotion of ultra-liberal values. The content of the Great Reset differs not too much from the content of globalisation, but we need to understand that globalisation is not just a technological, geopolitical or political process but also an ideological process that unites different levels. For example, this means that every country and every society is transformed into the West. That is very important.

Westernisation was a great part of this globalisation — because it is a projection of Western values and Western society on all of humanity. So, in globalisation, the West is taken as an example. The second level of globalisation is a projection of modernisation onto Westernisation. That means it is a more and more updated version of Western values — not the same Western values as they were yesterday. This is an ongoing process of some special transformation, a change of the Western values and paradigm. And this is important — it is a double process to update the West itself and project an updated version. This is a kind of postmodern combination of the Western and modern.

Modernisation should not only be applied to non-Western societies, but modernisation is also a domestic process in the West. So, globalisation is modernisation as well. The next level should be an ideological shift inside liberal globalisation because liberalism is also a process. It's not just a belief in something eternally stable, but it is the idea to liberate the individual from all forms of collective identity.

DEUTSCHE STIMME: *From what must the individual be liberated?*

ALEXANDER DUGIN: That is an historical process. It started with the liberation from the Catholic Church. After that, it was the liberation from the estates and from the belongingness to some society of the Middle Ages, and after that it was the liberation from the nation-state and from all kinds of artificial collective identities in the twentieth century. And after the defeat of Nazism and communism followed the next step — the liberation of man from collective gender identity. That was the mark of transition to a new kind of liberalism. So, gender politics is essential. It is not just secondary — it is something essentially embedded in this logic of development of liberalism.

So globalism is essentially and naturally associated with gender politics. That is extremely important. That is part of this modernisation of the liberal society itself. And the next point is the exchange of the human collective identity with the post-human collective identity. That is the political agenda for tomorrow that starts today; that is the main logic of globalisation; that is not just the opening of the borders. That is a very profound and multi-layered process of globalisation.

DEUTSCHE STIMME: *But what is new about the idea of the Great Reset?*

ALEXANDER DUGIN: New is the fact that the previous stages created oppositions of different kinds in non-Western societies, especially in the not-too-much Western, not-too-much modernised societies of Russia and China. Some aspects of the conservative features of these societies reacted against globalisation, and the defence of their sovereignty indicates that the great nuclear power Russia and the big economic power China have become obstacles in this process. At the same time, there appeared civilisations that have tried to react against the imposition of liberal, modernist and postmodernist values. That was an organic and natural reaction of civilisation against this ideological agenda.

At the same time, there were some economic errors and strategic defeats in geopolitics, like in the creation of the "Greater Middle East" project and the promotion of colour revolutions in the Arab world, which didn't deliver the successful results the globalists expected. So that was a chain of failures — failure after failure, and the last failure was the appearance of Trump.

So that was the revolt of American society that rejected this agenda. For example, they expressed their will to stay with yesterday's version of modernity, of liberalism, of democracy. They rejected the process of ongoing modernisation and update. So that was a kind of challenge from within — not from Putin, not from the rise of populism in Europe, but from a kind of split in American society itself.

All that put the globalists in a very special position. They tried to promote their agenda, which was based on the liberation of the individual from every kind of collective identity. They still wanted to project Westernisation; they still wanted to achieve stronger and stronger modernisation and thus achieve the destruction of every kind of identity in the West. But they encountered so many obstacles that they could not proceed in a normal way, so that is a kind of emergency signal that went off because there was an accumulation of the alternative powers and actors of different layers — civilisations, as well as sovereign, ideological, cultural, geopolitical, economic, but also political elements, which created a kind of front represented by Trump, Putin, growing Islam, Iran, China and in an economic way the Belt and Road Initiative, the wave of populism in Europe, a kind of split inside NATO, triggered by the independent and sovereign politics of Erdogan.

Everything went out of control. And there was a kind of growth of all these obstacles on the road to globalisation. So, that was a disaster, a catastrophe in the course of the last two decades, starting from 2000. This led to the end of the unipolar moment and a growing defeat. The globalists lost their positions everywhere, in every camp, and the final blow was delivered by Trump. So the American people joined this battle against the global agenda.

DEUTSCHE STIMME: *So, Donald Trump was a disaster from the viewpoint of the globalists?*

ALEXANDER DUGIN: Yes. Now they're in a critical position. When they speak about reset, that means the drastic and violent return to the continuation of their agenda. But it is not, as it seems, some kind of natural process of development of progress. Everything seemed almost granted twenty years ago, and now they have to fight for every element of this strategy because everywhere they encounter a growing resistance. So the globalists can't implement their strategy with the same means and the same methods anymore. And with that they mean three words: "Build Back Better". This is a kind of slogan, a catchphrase. Build back — back to before the anti-globalist moment — return to the 90s and be in a better position than back then.

DEUTSCHE STIMME: *So they want to go back in time in order to correct the errors made on the way to the New World Order?*

ALEXANDER DUGIN: Yes. This is a kind of call to arms to mobilise all the globalist forces in order to win the last battle on all the fronts, in order to break through everywhere. Defeating Trump is the first goal. They want to destroy Putin, kill Xi Jinping, change the government in Iran, poison Erdogan, discredit all varieties of European populism, finish the Islamic resistance, destroy all anti-globalist tendencies in Latin America! Not in a peaceful way, but by attacking with totalitarian means.

So, the Reset as a concept has the same content, but it presupposes totally new tools to implement the agenda, and I think the tools are now openly totalitarian. They try to impose censorship, they try to impose political pressure, concrete police measures against all who are on the other side. The Great Reset is the continuation (a kind of desperate continuation) of the failed globalist strategy against all this accumulation of obstacles. They couldn't accept their failure. It is the agony of a wounded dragon that is going to die, but can still kill because it's still alive. BBB — Build Back Better — that is the last cry of the dragon. "Kill all the enemies of the Open Society. The enemies of the Open Society should be killed — tortured if they win through the democratic process. We should abolish democracy", roars this dragon. "Destroy every obstacle. Humanity — let us destroy it. Put the poison in the vaccines. Let's do it!" That's the kind of eschatological fight — the last battle of globalisation.

And now we see that they use in the Great Reset all the means which were unthinkable in the previous stage. So, to finally answer the question "What is the Great Reset?" — it is nothing new. It is the same agenda of globalisation, the same ideology, the same values, the same process, but with totally new means. It is now clearly and openly totalitarian. Censorship, political repression, killing, fighting, demonisation of the enemy, denouncing all those who are against this as fascists, as maniacs, as terrorists, and dealing with them precisely in that way.

First of all, they view all their enemies as fascists. After that, they begin to kill them because they are fascists. Nobody investigates anything. That's just Bolshevism, just like in the Bolshevik Revolution or in the French Revolution. Everybody who is declared an enemy of the revolution should be exterminated. So that is extermination, and we see in the United States of America the first stages of this Great Reset. "The globalists have lost the elections? Let's destroy the elections! Kill all the protesters! Let's look at all those millions of people demonstrating as a small mob of maniacs and fascists!" So they destroy all kinds of reality checks. No more reality checks. Welcome to the totalitarianism of the Great Reset!

DEUTSCHE STIMME: *During the protests at the Capitol in Washington, you used the term "Great Awakening" as an antithesis to the Great Reset. What do you mean by that?*

ALEXANDER DUGIN: The Great Awakening is a term used spontaneously by American protesters, with Alex Jones and all the others. This was a concept that was born just recently, when the American people became more conscious of the true demonic nature of the globalists. That concerns first of all Americans that were under the illusion that everything was going more or less well, and that Democrats and Republicans inside the United States represented two wings of the same liberal democracy. The Great Awakening for them was the discovery that behind the mask of the Democratic Party was something totally different — a kind of coup d'état orchestrated by globalists, maniacs and terrorists.

They are ready to apply all kinds of totalitarian measures against the American people. That had been inconceivable and impossible before. It started with Trump during the four years of his presidency and climaxed in the election fraud — the stolen election, which was a clear picture of what is the Great Awakening. It is the understanding of the real nature of the Reset, of the globalists. The American people were hidden inside the American system, and now there are two completely different things — the American population (Trumpists, or normal Americans) and globalist America. And that is exactly the dividing line between the Great Reset and the Great Awakening.

DEUTSCHE STIMME: *Does the Great Awakening only have meaning for American patriots or also for us?*

ALEXANDER DUGIN: Whereas it is foremost about American patriots on the wave of the growing protests in the United States, we could compare the universal meaning of the Great Reset with a possible universal meaning of the Great Awakening, because the Great Reset is the summary of many civilisational tendencies that were prepared in previous centuries. It is not just the evil will of some group of idiots — no, it is the accumulation of negative results and stages of modernity. That is the negation of human nature: the creation of technical tools that become step by step the masters, and stop being tools. So, when the tool becomes the master, that changes everything; that is the Singularity moment — this alienation and the loss of human identities step by step, starting with the religious identity, with this ongoing nominalism, which pretends to destroy all kinds of collective identity. Now it is approaching the loss of human identity. You are still allowed to be human; it is optional. Tomorrow, being human will mean the same as being Trumpist or fascist, and so on. This is a very serious process, and that is the Great Reset.

The Great Awakening should be as universal as the Great Reset is. It should not be just a reaction of the American people, finally understanding the cultural identity of the ruling Democratic elites and the globalists in their country, because if the content of the Great Reset is so rich with meaning, if it is inscribed in what is called *Seinsgeschichte* by Heidegger, and the destiny of history—the ontological aspect of history—the Great Awakening should be an alternative. But it should be on the same level and not superficial. We are attacked by something which is globalisation, and globalism with something that is very deep metaphysically. It is technical, which is liberal, which is the modern and postmodern. There is a philosophy behind the globalists, and in order to fight this philosophy—which is almost fulfilled on a global scale, but experiencing more and more problems and failures—we need to capitalise on the alternative. For example, we need to revise the relations of the West against the East, or West against the rest. We need to consolidate the rest, from Asia to Europe, against the domination of this unique West. It will be the shift from unipolarity towards multipolarity, and the West should find its place inside this multipolar structure.

We need to destroy this Eurocentric/Western-centric attitude. We need to accept the plurality of civilisations, and that will be one of the many features of the Great Awakening. Secondly, we need to revise geopolitics. We need to elaborate multipolar geopolitics. Not only Western sea power against Eastern land power, but we need to identify sea power and land power in the West as well. The United States of America is a clear example of this new geopolitics. When there is land power, represented by the red states and by Republican Trumpists, there are coastal zones that represent sea power. That is a complete change of geopolitical vision. More than that, we need not only to fight against gender politics or dehumanisation, posthumanism or postmodernism. We need to revise, to return to what we have lost at the beginning of modernity. We need to re-appropriate the philosophical treasure of those authors and philosophers and metaphysicians and schools of thought that we have abandoned, and leave behind modernity. I think this is also a feature of the Great Awakening — the return to Plato; the return to antiquity; the return to the Middle Ages; the return to Aristotle; the return to Christianity; the return to traditional religions — all traditional religions. That is traditionalism.

The Great Awakening should be also an understanding of what we lost with modernity. So it should not be just a continuation of modernity or postmodernity. It should be a revision of modernity, a critical revision from the Left and from the Right. We need a complete revision of modernity itself. The Great Awakening is a kind of philosophical and metaphysical program — a manifesto that deals with the Great Reset as an absolute evil. It's a crystallisation of opposite value. It's not just a defence of Republicans against Democrats in the United States. It's a much deeper concept, and I think we're challenged now to create the common global front of the Great Awakening, where American protesters will be one wing and European populists will be the other wing. Russia in general will be the third; it will be an angelic entity with many wings — a Chinese wing, an Islamic wing, a Pakistani wing, a Shia wing, an African wing and a Latin American wing.

So we need to organise this Great Awakening by not only basing it on one dogma. Next step, different identities, and we need to find a place for them. This eschatology of the Great Awakening we find in Christian tradition. We find some special figures for that Second Coming of Christ for an apocalyptic fight against the Antichrist. The same in the Shia tradition of Islam, the same in the Sunni tradition of Islam, and there is the Indian tradition of Kali Yuga, the narrative about the end of Kali Yuga and the fight of the Tenth Avatar against the Demon of Perverted Time.

So we need another tradition, another understanding, another figure and other images for this Great Awakening, and everything coincides now. It shouldn't be just a political or economic rejection of the Great Reset. We need to understand the Great Reset as the biggest challenge. The Great Reset is a kind of conceptual chariot of the

Antichrist, and in order to fight against him, we need to have a spiritual weapon, not only a technical one. Material as well, but first of all spiritual. I think the Great Awakening should be an awakening of the spirit, an awakening of the thought, an awakening of the culture, an awakening of our almost lost roots, of our European, Eurasian, Asian or Islamic traditions. So I understand the Great Awakening, which has just begun, as the process of formation, creation and manifestation of this new spiritual understanding of history, and present and future, as well as organisation of the radical criticism against all of modernity, Western centrism, technological progress, and revision of the concept of time.

DEUTSCHE STIMME: *You mentioned the important topic of transhumanism, and you also wrote many articles on the object-oriented ontology of Reza Negarestani. Where do you see the danger resulting from these developments?*

ALEXANDER DUGIN: I think that object-oriented ontology is rather an enclosure, disclosure and manifestation of the real goal of modernity. It's a kind of final terminal point before which modernity acted in the name of man, and with object-oriented ontology we arrive at the point of the reality of the real goal, which was not the liberation of humanity but the annihilation of reality, the destruction of man, because after the death of God followed logically the death of man, and that was the hidden agenda that now is evident in object-oriented ontology. So, Reza Negarestani, Nick Land and Miaso and Harman, they invite us to quit, to leave humanity to get to the things themselves, to the object without the subjects. That is sort of the real agenda of materialism. So materialism was inspired by this object-oriented ontology that appeared at the end of materialism, not at its beginning. This is the logical consequence that they could have received earlier, but things are as they are, and in the history of *Dasein*, in the history of philosophy, object-oriented ontology came last. And so that is precisely the invitation, as Nick Land puts it, to destroy all of humanity and life on Earth. Before, it was just a black caricature of traditionalists against progressivists, because progress always affirmed that we are fighting for the liberation of humanity, for life on Earth, or human beings and freedom. Now appear a group of more progressive, more modernised, more futurist thinkers. "No, not at all. To be human is fascism. To be human is to impose the subjects on the objects". We need to liberate the objects from the subjects, from humanity, and, what is more interesting, explore the things as they are without man, without being a tool of man, without "being" at hand, in Heideggerian terminology.

They have arrived on the other side of the object. Where, supposedly, should be the void of nothing, they are discovering another subject. They are called the idiot gods of Lovecraft — the Old Ones — the figures that are beyond the objects, but at the same time inside of them. So the objects are liberated from the human subject, from humanity, and they open their hidden dimension, which is the real Devil. Object-oriented ontology is a kind of premonition or foreseeing of the advent of the philosophical Devil. So the philosophical Devil is here on the other side of the objects, and he appears little by little in academia, in gender studies, and that is the next step after analytical philosophy, which has prepared the territory for this non-human way of thought — artificial intelligence that could exist without humans and without life on earth.

So with object-oriented ontology, we're dealing with the real truth, not with a lie. For the first time, modernity has told the truth about itself. What was before was a lie of modernity. Modernity lied to everybody. "Oh, we're in favour of humanity. We're in favour of life. We are trying to liberate human beings and nature from the transcendental fascist God". That was a lie and not in favour of humanity but against humanity and God. The main idea was to liberate the Devil from the chains with which he was fixed in Hell. This was the liberation of the Devil, not of man, and now comes the moment to liberate the Devil from humanity and life. And that is object-oriented ontology that clearly, openly, explicitly affirms that, and they are object-oriented philosophers. They are closer to us traditionalists because we always saw in modernity this devilish, demonic aspect.

So for traditionalists, modernity was not neutral. Modernity from the very beginning was a satanic creation, and that is the main traditional line. Now there appear among the most progressivist philosophers schools of thought that say the same, but in favour of Satan. It is not Aleister Crowley or black masses or LaVey — the real black magic is modern science and modern culture. Modern civilisation is a kind of preparation for the advent of the Antichrist, and Islamic tradition identifies it as *Dajjal*. Christians see it as the Antichrist. I think that this appeal to Lovecraft, to black magic and to the extermination of mankind and nature is disclosed by Nick Land as the real nature of science and modernity as well, and this is why it serves the Great Awakening.

Object-oriented ontology is the other side of the Great Awakening, when our consciousness is awakened to the fact what progress in reality is. It mobilises our spiritual power, which awakens the rest of our human dignity, and that is the real fight. But it is much better to deal with people who tell the truth about their negative purposes and principles than with liars. So, inside of the lie, there appears the most radical truth about life. That is why I could not condemn it the same way that I hate analytical philosophy, positivism or the natural sciences of Newton or Galileo, which were a pure catastrophe and a lie about nature and humanity. For example, I hate Biden and Kamala Harris, but I could not hate Reza Negarestani or Nick Land or Harman who are real and conscious Satanists. So better to deal with the reality as it is than with all these lies. If, for example, a progressivist in the United States would declare that they serve Satan, and Satan should return, it's much easier for us to deal with him. So I always prefer the truth, even when the truth is very dark and very terrible. I always prefer the truth to the comfortable lie that tries to seep into our thoughts. The evil helps to awaken because it's terrible, and I think that what Americans are now experiencing with Kamala Harris and the Democrats is the real horror. The more horror, the better, I think.

DEUTSCHE STIMME: *This leads us to the conference you organised just recently, called Wozu Philosophen in dürftiger Zeit? (What are philosophers for in a destitute time?) There you presented the concept of the radical subject, which was born of the thought of Aristotle and Johannes Tauler. Please explain to our readers what it is all about.*

ALEXANDER DUGIN: This is the most important point because in the radicalisation of the Great Reset against the Great Awakening, the concept of the subject is in the centre of the battle. Conservatives are trying to save the human subject, and the progressivists are now openly trying to destroy it in favour of post-human/non-human artificial intelligence, technological cyberspace — cyber-ontology. So the problem of the subject is in the centre, because the partisans of the radical object are not satisfied anymore to define human beings as masters of their bodies. They try to regard man as measure. That is why they try to decipher the genome, why they try to improve the DNA. They treat humans as measure. That is modern medicine, modern vaccines, modern technology, and so on. That is the main point — that man is some kind of measure, and he is not the perfect measure. And the main point of this conference was that radical self is precisely the idea that we cannot save and defend if we accept the manner in which it was understood and presented, during the modern age and modern philosophy. It was already a mutilated subject, which was an insufficient subject. The subject cut from its root, and in order to save the secondary peripheral subject, we need to restore this subject — return it to its roots. What was not inside, but even more inside the inner world — it's a kind of inner transcendence where we should arrive in order to save the subject that was abandoned and destroyed completely. So that is a very important thing that we have forgotten. We have forgotten one of the segments of this way inside ourselves to consider what is inmost — *homo intimus* in Latin. We consider our intellect as something which Aristotle considered as passive intelligence. We have forgotten our active intellect, starting from the Middle Ages with the Scholastic tradition. My idea — a return to, or to restore, this radical subject. That is important. This active intellect, in order to radically fight against all those who challenge all subjects. In my opinion, we could not defend and save the non-radical subject, which is still here, without the restoration of the radical subject, which disappeared many centuries ago from the field of philosophy. So, the rediscovery of active intelligence inside of our souls and inside of our heart is much the same as a rediscovery of the absolute spirit in Hegel and Schelling, or Fichte, with the "absolute I". I think that this is the way to decipher — through German classical philosophy, which was perverted by left Hegelianism, by Marxism and some other application of it. We need to rediscover the dignity of philosophy as such with Heidegger, first of all, as well as with other German philosophers. We should rediscover Aristotle using phenomenological methods. We need to re-evaluate modernity in philosophy as the stages of the loss of this radical subject, starting from appending this instance of image in St. Augustine, Dietrich von Freiberg and philosophers such as Tauler, Meister Eckardt or von Suso, as well as Paracelsus and Jakob Böhme. All of them had a clear understanding and experience of this radical self, and I think this is not just a special branch of philosophy, not something arbitrary. It is in the centre; it is inevitable; it is the main problem. So, the main problem, in order to save humanity, is to save the radical subject that was, for many hundred years, forgotten and marginalised in philosophy. Only with this rehabilitation of active intellect can we be prepared to bring the final battle to object-oriented philosophy and progressivism. So, the main theoretical weapon of the Trumpists in the Great Awakening should be philosophy. German philosophy, Greek philosophy, traditional Western philosophy — they are fighting for the West. They are fighting for Indo-European culture. Therefore, they should know the principles of it. Otherwise, the fight is lost from the very beginning. So, I think that without this layer of radical subject, we cannot dream about victory.

The Great Awakening: The Future Starts Now

January 2021

I N H I S T O R Y we had and still have many opposite issues and con-flicts with the U.S. on a geopolitical level. We fight on different sides of conflicts on many occasions. But what is going on in the U.S. now is another question. *That is a question of principles.*

Half of the U.S. is under totalitarian rule by the other half. There has arrived areal left-liberal dictatorship. And in such a situation we are obliged to express full solidarity with the oppressed half.

There were no elections this time; there was a coup d'état ac-complished by a conspiracy of the illegitimate elites. The American presidency was hijacked. Now the U.S. is under control of an extrem-ist junta. Welcome to Maidan or the Third World.

But this is the first time that the globalists have used the same scenario of colour revolution, including a stolen election, fraud and disinformation campaigns, *at home*. So their face is now fully revealed and clearly seen. Before, they approved such tactics by "American na-tional interests". Now Americans themselves are victims. It is a logical conclusion. If you start to use lies and violence, there comes a time when you cannot use it anymore — at a certain point, the lies will use you.

The main struggle is now clearly *international.* The globalists *vs* anti-globalists is today much more important than Russians *vs* Americans, or the West *vs* the East, or else Christians *vs* Muslims.

So our name is Ashli Babbitt. Yes, she participated in imperialist wars of the U.S. But her sacrifice on 6 January 2021 is something more than a last service to the American state and the American people. She gave her life for real freedom and real justice. And freedom and justice are *universal values.* Russian as well as American, Muslim as well as Christian, Western as well as Eastern.

Our fight is not against America anymore. The America we knew doesn't exist anymore. The split of American society is henceforth irreversible. We are in the same situation everywhere — inside the U.S. and outside. So it is the same fight on a global scale.

We should revise our attitude to technology. Microsoft, Google, Twitter, Apple, YouTube, Facebook and so on are not just commercial — presumably "neutral" — *tools. They are ideological weapons and machines of surveillance and censorship. We need to destroy them.* We need to accomplish the great exit from the technosphere controlled by globalist madmen. The question is whether to dismantle technology in general (the eco-solution, which we should not disregard or decline too hastily) or develop independent networks free from the control of ideologically biased shackles. We can move meanwhile in both directions simultaneously. The same with media. They are proving now really to be the message. And it is a *unilateral message.*

I disagree with many observers that consider the assault on the Capitol as a provocation and fifth column job. No. That was a *symmetric response* by the other half of America, totally humiliated by a stolen election and the shameless fraud of the Democrats. The Trumpists have shown that there is *no left-liberal privilege to organise mimetic wars and to use violence for political ends.* If you start to use violence, you should expect the same in return. Antifa and BLM started the riots. Capitol Hill was the logical response. We are strong enough to seize *by force* Congress, which is occupied *by frauds and dirty tricksters,* with the fake votes of dead people and ballots that nobody ever sent.

Now our fight obtains really global dimensions: *we are at war with the Democrats — with only half of the U.S. — not with the U.S. as such.* That fact changes everything. The *Heartland* is above all. The American Heartland as well as the Eurasian one. The geopolitics of the 2020 election show us the boundaries of two Americas — a coastal, Atlanticist, ultra-liberal and globalist blue one and a conservative, traditionalist Heartland painted red. The *blue* perversion against the *red* normality.

The real struggle begins just now. The fear Democrats felt during the peaceful protests on Capitol Hill will be a reminder for all of them. Seeing simple American people — the dispossessed majority, silent and "deplorable" — coming to Congress — that was the moment of truth. And deputies hid themselves under benches... The real "deplorables" are these cowards. They grasped in this marvellous moment that they are not safe anymore anywhere. Welcome into our skin. From now on, the Democrats will be attacked worldwide. They should know: we observe them exactly as they do; we will follow them exactly as they do; we will gather information and create dossiers on all the Democrats, globalists and their puppets, exactly as they do. From now on, any connection with Democrats and their proxies will be considered *collaborationism* and participation in crimes against humanity. They killed thousands and hundreds of thousands outside the U.S. But evil doesn't recognise limits. It is always based on hubris. *So they started to kill Americans themselves.* Ashli Babbitt is just the beginning. They are planning a real genocide inside the U.S. this time. And it has already began.

There are only two parties in the world: the globalist party of the Great Reset and the anti-globalist party of the Great Awakening. And nothing in the middle. Between them there is the abyss. It wants to be filled with oceans of blood. The blood of Ashli Babbitt is the first drop.

The fight becomes universal. The Democratic Party of the U.S. and its globalist proxies — including all high tech industries and Big Finance — as of now, are a clear embodiment of *absolute evil.*

The great evil made its nest on American soil. From the centre of Hell starts now the Last Revolt, the *Great Awakening.*

Last remark: Trumpism is much more important than Trump himself. Trump has the honour of having started the process. Now we need to go further.

Theoretical Principles of the Great Awakening (Based on the Fourth Political Theory)

18 January 2021

TWENTY-ONE POINTS

1. Liberalism is in decay

- Now we can easily observe that the global world order is in decay. **Globalism is collapsing.** We see, for example, a real agony in the Unites States. The threat of President Trump — who is much more moderate in regards to the global liberal agenda — is experienced by globalists as something fatal, something existential. Globalists are trying to destroy the United States in order to promote their candidate, to save their agenda at any price.

- **Trump has called cancel culture a new kind of postmodern totalitarianism.** For example, the *New York Times* has declared the necessity to cancel Aristotle (https://www.nytimes.com/2020/07/21/opinion/should-we-cancel-aristotle.html). We are dealing with the clear totalitarian face of the liberal ideology. **It is a liberal dictatorship, because it demands to cancel history** — Plato, Aristotle, the Middle Ages, modern authors, modern philosophies ... anything that doesn't coincide with the more and more narrowing criteria of radical and totally intolerant liberalism.

- These are clear signs of totalitarianism. The Nazis (National Socialists) demanded to cancel Jews. The Soviet totalitarianism (socialist totalitarianism) demanded to cancel dissidents. **Now, the liberal ideology demands to cancel everything — or almost everything, except Black Lives Matter, Soros' LGBT+, and some chosen groups of minorities, at the price of prohibiting everybody else.** So, that is agony.

2. Liberalism and its alternatives

- What is agony? Liberalism is agony.

- First political theory: Liberalism

- Second political theory: Communism

- Third political theory: Fascism — or National Socialism

- **Liberalism has won over its rivals in the twentieth century (communism and fascism).**

- **These three theories represent political modernity — Western political modernity.**

- **The agony of liberalism includes the approaching end of Western political modernity, because neither communism nor fascism could be regarded as real alternatives to liberalism.**

- **Communism and fascism have a common basis with liberalism:** Materialism — Atheism — Progressivism — A purely materialistic approach to the human being.

- **We will miss the opportunity of the growing crisis** — fueled by the impossibility of globalist structures to deal with the coronavirus (another sign of the collapse of liberalism) —, **if we choose** to oppose it with communism and fascism, because they are alternatives of the past. And they belong to the same family of Western modern ideologies.

- So, the Fourth Political Theory is an invitation to use this window of historical opportunity (represented by the agony of liberalism as the first political theory) **to overcome what is common to all forms of political modernity — to overcome the philosophical, metaphysical, political and ideological field of political modernity.**

3. The Fourth Political Theory vs. Western modernity

- The Fourth Political Theory is an invitation to search for the alternative to this falling liberalism in decay, which intended to be the main and unique, the one and only political ideology from Fukuyama's moment of *The End of History and the Last Man* (1992) until now.

- After the end of communism and fascism in the twentieth century, liberalism became the only political ideology, which intended to be a kind of universal language — something totally imposed, with the free market, liberal democracy, parliamentarianism, individualism, technology, icon culture and LGBT+ ethics. All that was regarded as universal. And now this universality is ending.

- The Fourth Political Theory is an invitation to critique and fight the first political theory, neither from the socialist or communist position, nor from the nationalist-fascist or National Socialist position — because both belong to the past. This is an invitation to overcome Western political modernity by fighting liberalism, because it still exists.

4. Why is liberalism the absolute evil?

- We precisely choose liberalism to be the representation and symbol of absolute evil because it is still here, and **liberals still intend to organise the world under the rule of the liberal transnational elite.**

- **Liberalism is worse than communism and fascism not only from the theoretical point of view. It is worse because it exists here still. Communism and fascism belong to the past — they are chimeras, they are just leftovers, residues of political history.**

- **So, first of all, we need to fight liberalism.** We need to bring this lasting decay to the end, we need to overcome liberalism, we need to finish with liberalism — with the open society, with human rights, with all the products of this Soros-style liberal system based on individualism, materialism, progressivism, on the total alienation of the people and extinction of social links.

- **Individualism is the last word of liberalism. So, we need to finish with the concept of individualism.**

5. Communism and fascism are the traps

- We should not come to the past alternatives. **We shouldn't fall into the trap of communism or fascism. We need to imagine something radically different — not only from liberalism, but from Western political modernity taken altogether. This is the Fourth Political Theory — this is what it's all about.**

- **Today, our main enemy is represented by liberalism, by the open society, by Soros-funded groups of liberal terrorists** — which could be regarded as leftists or far-left fascists. And others: liberals are trying to use religious and ethnic groups. **For example, when fighting Islam as a sacred religious tradition, globalists**

are using some Muslims in order to destroy the European identity. When fighting against all kinds of national identity, they use some ethnic identities (for example, Uyghurs, Ukrainians) in order to destabilise the alternative poles that don't belong to their vision of a unipolar, liberal world. **They are cynical in that sense; they are hypocrites — they can use something they criticise if they need to. They have a double morality.**

- **But the main idea of fighting liberalism is to fight all Western political modernity. That is the enemy. The Fourth Political Theory invites everybody to fight.**

6. The name of the enemy is Western modernity

- **The name of the enemy has absolute importance.** If we name the enemy as the modern Western political ideologies or Western political modernity, we already are on the right path.

- **We don't invite people to fight against the West.** Not at all. The West is not an enemy.

- **We don't invite people to fight against modernity** as such — for example, the contemporary state of affairs in some societies. **Because we have different societies, different civilisations that exist in the modern world and don't belong to Western modernity.** We can actually live in the modern world outside Western political modernity.

- So, we are challenging neither the West nor modernity: we are challenging Western modernity. **And that's a kind of form based on the anti-Christian, anti-spiritual, anti-traditional, anti-sacred turn in Western history that coincided — not by chance — with colonialism, the beginning of the Enlightenment, and so on. This modern era of the scientific, materialist, colonialist period of Western history is the evil; this is the problem.**

7. Against capitalism, slavery and Enlightenment

- We have identified our main enemy as **Western political modernity**, or **Western modernity** in general — in the philosophical, scientific, geopolitical and economic senses. **It coincides with capitalism, because capitalism, materialism, atheism and colonialism re-introduced slavery after hundreds of years of the non-existence of slavery in Western Christian culture. Slavery was reintroduced by Western political modernity.**

- **Sometimes it seems that slavery in colonial times, in America and Africa, was a phenomenon continued from the ancient tradition of the pre-modern West. Not at all. It was a completely new institution — a modern institution.** Modern slavery is the path of the so-called "democratic liberal" modernity. People fighting colonialism should understand it very well: they are fighting Western political modernity.

- **That new concept of slavery was based on race and biological aspects, and based on progress.** Because there was no reasonable explanation for using Black or coloured people as slaves apart from progress. That was a new concept of slavery based on measuring progress. **Progressivism was the main moving power behind slavery.**

- **In order to liberate the consequences of slavery and colonialism, we need to extinguish Western political modernity. This is the only way.** If we wrongly project slavery outside the Western political bourgeois and capitalist modernity, we will be led to the wrong conclusion. **The whole phenomenon was created, explained and funded by Western political modernity.**

8. Inspiration from the East

- **How can we get out of this epistemological field of Western political modernity?** If we focus on the name *Western political modernity*, we already have a solution. In order to get out of these boundaries, **we invite you to go beyond the West. So, welcome to the East. Welcome to the non-Western civilisations.**

- **Welcome to Islam, welcome to India, welcome to the great ancient Chinese civilisation, welcome to Africa, welcome to the archaic societies.** All these forms of civilisations could be our examples to follow.

- **We should consider Western history as only one branch of the history of humanity.** If we reject the pretensions of Westerners' universalism, **we could rediscover the values of Chinese political ideas, Islamic political ideas, Christian Orthodox political thought — Eastern, not Western, which is a completely different form of political thought.** We could rediscover Indian tradition, we could rediscover archaic people, and not judge them from the point of view of progress or technological development.

- **People in all forms, living in all kinds of societies, are still human — maybe more human than our technological civilisation. We should rediscover the multiplicity of all kinds of cultures and societies, and we should accept them**. Accept the most archaic people, the most archaic societies and tribes living outside the so-called "civilisation" as an example to follow, maybe, or to discover, to study, **something that we need to understand first, not judge or try to bring within the criteria of Western political modernity**.

- **We are rediscovering every kind of civilisation outside the West. And that is great. We have this immense amount of political thought, cultural thought, philosophy, religion — outside** the West. **And we can take them as a source of inspiration to create something new.** We can propose something non-Western and take it as a guiding star for the Fourth Political Theory.

- **Obviously, we cannot reach some new kind of universalism.** And we shouldn't, we don't need that. **We need to open the perspectives for each civilisation, each culture to create their own political future,** apart from something that is imposed as inevitable, as a destiny by colonial Western modernity.

- First of all, the invitation is geographical. We should recognise the value of political thought outside the West. For example, Russian Eurasianists have remarked that Austrian philosopher Kelsen's study on the universal history of law is entirely dedicated to Roman law. Just a few pages are dedicated to all the other non-Western legal systems. That doesn't mean that Roman law is evil. **There are non-Roman law systems outside the Western civilisation — and that is great. We have Islamic law, Chinese law, the Confucianist tradition, Indian law, besides some archaic systems of legality and legitimacy. We need to consider them all.**

- **All civilisations can be inspired by their own political thought. That is the meaning of the Fourth Political Theory.** After the end of liberalism (which is approaching), **we need to rehabilitate non-Western political systems.** These systems could seem to Westerners as terrible, not civil, or awful, but that is not an argument. **Westerners should worry about their own civilisation, which is only one kind of civilisation among many others. And nobody can judge the others.** Nobody — neither Soros, nor Bill Gates, nor Hillary Clinton, nor Washington, nor Brussels, nor Moscow, nor Riyadh, nor New Delhi, nor Beijing.

- **Nobody can judge the other. There is no universal criterion in political thought, and that's the main principle of the Fourth Political Theory.**

9. True universalism is based on the plurality of subjects

- In order to develop a positive meaning for a postliberal world order, **we should recognise this as the main law: all civilisations can establish their own political systems outside any universal paradigm** — above all, outside the modern Western political paradigm, accepted or imposed as something universal. **Democracy, liberalism, human rights, LGBT+, robotisation, progress, digitalisation and cyberspace are optional. They are not universal values.** There are no universal values, except the value upon which all kind of civilisations could agree.

- We lack a real international order, because we lack the full-scale subjects that could establish such law. **Now, we are still in colonisation. There is only one subject: the modern Western liberal subject, which tries to impose its own values as a universal formal order over all others. And this is absolutely wrong. We are fighting precisely against this pretension.** The West is the West. The West is not all. The West is a part of the whole. Westerners are a part of humanity. The West can be accepted or rejected — that depends on the free decision of other civilisations. The West is one civilisation among many others.

- **That's why non-Western political thought is so important. The real universal history of law should include all legal systems of all existing civilisations** — the serious part of Confucianism, the serious part of Indian political thought, the great part of Islamic law, the great part of Byzantine law, the great part of the various archaic systems of law.... Each archaic tribe can create their own system, and we should be very attentive to that. And, of course, the great part of Roman law. Yet, we could also include modern Western political thought — but that should be a small part of the whole political thought of humanity.

- **We should insist on this redistribution of the system of values. This is a path to get out of Western political modernity. We should recognise the full-scale dignity of non-Western political thought**. This is very concrete: in each civilisation we can easily find a huge amount of political treaties, ideas, schools.... But we are ignoring them totally, dealing with the open society and its enemies (Karl Popper, Hayek, or Karl Marx) as universal thinkers or systems. Yes, they are more or less interesting. But, **compared to Confucianism, Indian political thought and Islamic political thought, liberalism, Marxism and Western nationalism are very poor**. They are just possible forms of political thought — a small proportion, a very arrogant proportion of humanity. **They are just a small part, not the whole**. And this is extremely important.

10. The West is just a part of the Rest

- **We need to restore the dignity of all non-Western political philosophies, including Africa, India and the Americas. Including great and developed civilisations, as well as the small archaic societies of Oceania.**

- **We need to accept humanity as humanity** — not the West and the Rest. We should reverse the position: the Rest is the name of humanity, and the West is the name of the disease on the body of humanity. The Rest is the centre, not the West.

- Now, **we are living in a system where the modern West is the unique pole (unipolar) and intends to establish the rule for the Rest. We need to organise the global geopolitical human revolution against that.** We should evenly distribute the status of the subject between the Rest. The West is part of the Rest — a small part of the Rest.

- We should not punish the West. We should put it within its normal historical, organic borders — nothing else. **You are Western? Alright, but you are not universal**. You strongly believe in human rights, LGBT+? It's up to you. It is your decision, not mine. It is not necessary. We could prohibit gay marriages or gay pride — that is absolutely our own right, and that is the highest decision we could take. Or we could let it happen...

- **Nothing should be universally condemned or justified. Everything depends on the balance of the decision made by each civilisation.**

- In order to establish the world order on this principle, we need to reject the claim of Western political modernity to establish universal rule. **Non-Western societies should be put first.** We should extinguish Western consensus; **there's no such thing as Western consensus. There is regime, there is colonisation, there is occupation — this is the Western imperial liberalism we should fight against.**

11. The West itself should be liberated from modernity

- **This is very important; we shouldn't blame the West — we should blame the modern West.** And that is totally different, because not only many peoples of the world are colonised and exploited by Western modernity: the identity of Western culture (of Western civilisation, of Western society) is also hijacked by modernity. And now, with the flourishing of the cancel culture, we see how it works. **Modern-day liberals are trying to cancel the very principles of Western identity. Cancel Aristotle, cancel Plato, cancel Hegel, cancel Nietzsche, cancel Heidegger — demonizing everything in great Western thought and culture — everything that doesn't fit into the narrow limits of this radically** intolerant left-liberal ideology. **Everything is judged as fascism, as something unacceptable.**

- **The modern West more and more destroys the principles of the West (pre-modern West). So, we need to liberate the West.** Not only liberate the Rest from the West; but, at the same time, we need to liberate the West from modernity. Because modernity tries to cancel the origins, the sources of Western identity. Now, it is quite open. **Everybody is colonised by Western political modernity. Not only the non-Western cultures and civilisations — the West itself is colonised by modernity.**

- **We need to liberate the West. We need to liberate Plato, Aristotle, Graeco-Roman antiquity. We need to restore the dignity of the Christian pre-modern societies — political thought, cultural values, philosophies, metaphysics...** We need to restore the heritage of the pre-modern West, which is on the way to being totally cancelled by a new purge from liberalism.

- **We should be united in the global revolution against Western political modernity.** But we should understand that we are not fighting against the West. **We are fighting against the regime of modernity.**

- **Modernity is anti-West. It's not the West. It's a deviation of Western history, based on a total misunderstanding of its own self. Western modernity is the disease.** It's a Western disease — but, first of all, it kills the West itself. So, we need to help the West to be free from modernity.

- **We need to liberate Europe and the United States from liberalism. We should support all kinds of popular movements and tendencies that try to restore social justice and liberate the people from the liberal political elites that promote more and more modernisation, liberalism, suicide.** Because now postmodern Western education is focused on the total destruction of any kind of Western values. **That's a new barbarism. Liberals don't bring culture, they bring barbarism. This cancel culture (which includes LGBT+, Black Lives Matter, and other feminist tendencies) is like a call to cancel all other kinds of culture. It is the genocide of the Western culture.**

- Modernity is not Western. It is a disease, a modern disease that kills Western identity. And it is not a human enemy that causes this disease — it is caused by a change in the register of existence.

- **We need to finish with capitalism, Western modernity, materialism, modern science — all kinds of political, cultural, philosophical fruits of modernity. And that is not nihilism, not at all.** Because by extinguishing modernity, we will be able to perceive the huge heritage of Graeco-Roman culture (which is cancelled now, or in the process of being radically cancelled). **We will discover the roots of Western identity: the spiritual, religious, philosophical, political roots** — not this kind of deviation and perversion we are dealing with through political modernity.

- **Not only should the world be decolonised, the West itself should be decolonised and restored to its real dignity — as one great civilisation among other great civilisations.**

- So, it is not against the West. **It is against liberalism and globalism, against Western political modernity.**

12. Postmodernity viewed from the Right

- **The Fourth Political Theory is an invitation to go forward, to go ahead. We can take inspiration from the past, but we are living in the present. We shouldn't return to the past exactly as it was — we need to make a step ahead, forward, not many steps backward.** The past should be considered as an eternal example, as Platonic ideas, as the being that inspires us. **But we are dealing**

with time, and modern time is the catastrophe. It's the time of the decay, the collapse, the final catastrophe. So, we need to go further.

- **We could use some methods of postmodernity in order to deconstruct Western political modernity. There are two parts in postmodernism. First, there is very legitimate criticism of the violent and perverted part of Western political modernity as totalitarianism.** We could agree with this postmodern criticism. **But there is a second part of postmodernism: the moral continuation of modernity — an agreement with its call for further liberation, egalitarianism and other subjects of the left-liberal morality. In that moral aspect, postmodernity is much worse than modernity.** But we need to separate these two parts. We could accept and use the criticism and the deconstruction process of the the modernity, and reject the moral solidarity ways that are proper for postmodernism. We need to have a kind of "right" postmodernism — postmodernity viewed from the Right. Not the political or economic Right. This word is only used to differentiate it from the left-liberal use of postmodernity to destroy more and more the Western and global human identity. So, we need to focus on the deconstruction process of Western political modernity without sharing the moral presumptions of postmodernity.

13. Coronavirus: globalism has totally failed

- **Now, coronavirus is the plague — a kind of eschatological sign (this is very important), as well as the symbol of the total incapacity of the globalists to manage a problem like an epidemic. This is a clear sign of the end of globalisation.**

- **Coronavirus and the lockdown have shown how fragile the globalist system is.** And when we are challenged by a serious threat, we immediately close the borders. Closing the borders is a short-term solution for anything. And maybe, still living in partial lockdown, we could learn a very important thing from that: **opening or removing borders is not a universal solution. It can be useful or harmful, so it is not a universal solution. No solution is universal when we're dealing with the liberal elites.**

- The liberal elites trying to put out fire with oil is suicide. An example is what's happening now in the United States. Democrats are losing their legitimate struggle for power against Trump, so they are trying to use a civil war as an argument to get their results. This is suicide — the politics of suicide.

14. Liberalism: extremism, crime, suicide, hatred

- **What all liberals do today is suicide. So, we should stop them, we should overcome them. No liberalism — it must be put aside. Liberalism is today's name for fascism. If in the past we demonised fascism, now the word liberal should be an insult. If you are liberal, you are subhuman, you are less than human, you are a diseased creature, a perverted creature. And you are a criminal, because you are fueling civil war, social injustice, occupation, colonisation, dehumanisation. Liberalism is a crime, a crime against humanity — worse than fascism and communism.** That doesn't mean we should restore fascism or communism. They were totalitarian regimes. We should put them aside as well. They belong to the past. And liberalism is the real danger, the real criminal system of world order that still exists.

- **To be anti-fascist or anti-communist is to fight with the shadow of the past. The real challenge is to be anti-liberal.** Today, there are them and us. "Them" are the liberals, and they are not only against Russian, Chinese, Muslim and European patriots — **they are against North-Americans, Latin-Americans, Africans, Europeans and everybody else**. They are alienated from their own society. They have no legitimacy to rule, because they are usurpers, exploiters, killers. **To be liberal is to be a killer.**

- **That's how precisely the Fourth Political Theory understands the situation.** And that is the frame of the debate we would like to have with you at the First International Congress on the Fourth Political Theory.

15. The Fourth Political Theory and the new educational project

- Finally, we need to act — to put these considerations (if you share them, if you agree with them) in some kind of practice. **And the most important and central practice is in education. Because it is through education that liberals penetrate our society, pervert our children, destroy the very principles of cultures and countries, destroy and dissolve identities.**

- **The main struggle should be at the university level. We suggest using this global lockdown to promote an online structure of alternative education,** outside Western political modernity. Religious, Christian, Islamic, Hinduist, Buddhist — all kinds of non-modern Western approaches to education.

16. Program for the first caste: Brahmans, philosophers

- **At the level of education, there are three types of people we are addressing. The first type is the small minority of the global population that is inclined to follow philosophy, religion and theology.** And we should satisfy their demand by giving them the full picture of the spiritual culture we are going to lose with liberals. We need to save this treasure of religious, traditional, ancient, and modern wisdom. We need to save and preserve this spiritual heritage. **That's our mission: to satisfy the need of the thinking persons — philosophers of the world — by giving them access to the real content of the spiritual tradition of different religions and different cultures.**

- **We need to promote this traditionalist education — including metaphysics, theology, medieval tradition, as well as non-Western systems of thought.** And all kinds of philosophical tendencies that formally belong to the modern West, but that are different from it — for example, **German classical philosophy starting with Fichte, Schelling, Hegel, or Nietzsche, Heidegger,** the Conservative Revolution, traditionalism, Italian thought, artistic realms less affected by the modern Western capitalist and liberal principles....

- **All that should be saved and transformed into something accessible to the people throughout the world. Why is it so important? Because in the Western type of education, precisely these things are disappearing before our eyes.** Today, there is no classical education in the best high schools and universities. They are losing this heritage. They are more and more involved in the cancel culture. **They are trying to cancel everything in education.**

- **Using the Indian term, this is the Fourth Political Theory project at the level of the Brahmans — philosophers, priests, sacerdotes, intellectuals. It's a kind of a very special engagement for highly intellectual people. It couldn't be for the masses. It is for these isolated individuals.** We need to pay attention to them, we need to satisfy their needs. If the liberal system of education advances, they will be totally alienated. And that will affect not only Western universities, but also Eastern universities, which only imitate the Western pattern.

17. Program for the second caste: Kshatriyas, warriors, activists

- But we also need to make an educational call for the political elite: the fighters, the Kshatriyas, the warriors. And they cannot be satisfied only with knowledge, they should put knowledge into practice. They should participate in a special online educational program in order to create warrior knowledge — i.e., knowledge on how to fight our enemy. To do so, they need special qualities. We should restore the values of the kinds of people who are potential heroes. They are totally excluded from postmodernity, from liberalism — they don't exist anymore.

- It was not by chance that Western political modernity has promoted the eradication of the first two estates: the priests, and the aristocracy — the warriors. Capitalism came to destroy these two kinds of human personalities. Now, we've arrived at the last stage of eradication of Brahmans and Kshatriyas throughout the world. We need to help them restore themselves and fulfill their existential and metaphysical missions.

- So, we need to create a network for the modern Kshatriyas to fight liberalism, the unipolar world order and Western political modernity — but not to fight each other. This is very important. The Fourth Political Theory invites all Kshatriyas not to fight against each other — for example, Chinese against Indians, Indians against Pakistanis, Shias against Sunnis, Christians against Muslims, Africans against White people, or one nation against another nation. Because this is the strategy of the liberals. They want to divide and rule (divide et impera). And when they spot some warrior spirit ascending in society, they try to manipulate it and orientate it against other potential rivals, competitors, or enemies of the open society. We shouldn't fall in this trap, either. We need to promote solidarity among all Kshatriyas of the world.

- **First of all, we should finish with globalism; and after that, we shall solve our mutual problem.** But, this common network of Kshatriyas, warriors, heroes, is very important. **We need to provide education for all these Kshatriyas based on solidarity between the warrior type of men and women.** Because this type of human personality is distributed evenly among men and women. **We should not be arrogant with women — we should rehabilitate the traditional dignity of women.**

- **In political modernity today, women are seen as goods, because the capitalist-materialist logic prevails. We need to liberate women for their own destiny — which may be linked to the philosophical type.** It is a rare case, but philosophy is rare; it is a very special feature of the human being. And, as Plato said, it is rarely found among men — but it is also rarely found among women. It is rare as such. **Men who are totally devoted to philosophy and metaphysics are rare, but women who are so are also rare.**

- **We need to restore the dignity of women and give them access to the Fourth Political education under the same conditions as men. The difference in the metaphysical structure of the soul is much more important than gender difference.** So, after creating the Brahman education open to men and women worldwide, we should promote a network of modern Kshatriyas, also open to women, in order to fight against the modern world, and not among each other.

18. Program for the third caste: Vaishyas, peasants, countrymen

- But all that is dedicated to a small minority of the global population, because the Brahmans (the thinkers, philosophers, intellectuals) are rare; and the warriors — the real heroes — are rare as well. And what to do with the huge mass of the population that is also the victim of liberals? What could we propose outside of this elitist approach? **The main idea is to organise a third level of education for the absolute majority of the population, which should be linked to the restoration of the traditional family and the traditional way of life with agriculture. Peasantry is the answer.**

- **First of all, the European peasantry was destroyed by capitalism.** The people who intended to be third estate bourgeois were not representatives of the real third estate in the European tradition, because the third estate was precisely represented by the peasants. The **European peasantry — that was the third estate in European societies. It wasn't represented by traders.** The traders were the parasites, intermediates between the higher classes of society and the huge ocean of peasantry.

- **We need to restore the system of self-sufficient agricultural societies based on small villages.** The coronavirus lockdown has showed us how important it is to have access to nutrition to satisfy the simplest needs of people. This will be more and more important in the future.

19. Exit from cities: great return to the earth

- **We need to focus on this new tendency of returning to the earth, in which the majority of the population returns to the agricultural practice. We need to promote, help and support the exodus from big cities — that's very important.**

- Big cities are artificial constructions of the modern West. **Big industrial cities should be extinguished — the population should abandon them and live a real life on the earth, because only the earth gives us real life and real access to being.**

- **We need to create a third level of education focused on the new peasantry.** People can join our Fourth Political Theory network online, but **it should be organised outside the big cities, on the basis of traditional families** — without the perverts from big cities.

- **We need to go to the earth. And it doesn't mean returning to the past: it is the only way to save humanity from this real disease represented by posthumanism and new technology** that tries to manipulate human genes, to transform us, to mark us with artificial substances in order to control and cancel our culture from our veins and our souls. We should fight against this globalisation.

- For the vast majority of the population, the Fourth Political Theory proposes the return to the earth — that is, return to the people, return to the origins, return to the sources. It could be **a movement of massive creation of agri-cooperation: agricultural communities linked throughout the world by the system and structure provided by the Fourth Political Theory network.**

- **We need to educate the new peasantry. We need to help them restore their native traditions, their roots, their ancestors, their cultures. Because agricultural life was full of symbolism and sacredness.** Romanian traditionalist Mircea Eliade was a representative of this very rich peasant sacredness. He could be a representative of the third estate traditionalism for the new peasantry. We could develop this idea in our debate.

20. The people: the main subject of the Fourth Political Theory

- **We should promote the people as the main subject of the Fourth Political Theory, for the people always presupposes the relations with the earth — in the concrete, symbolic and sacred senses.** So, Nietzsche's words "My brethren, stay loyal to the earth" should be taken into consideration. Because **the earth for the**

people is the being — it is not an alienated substance to be used for material needs. **The earth is sacred**.

- **This return to the earth from the cities, this abandonment of the big cities should be an existential and metaphysical move to return to the being. The mission of the Fourth Political Theory is to promote this process.**

21. The Fourth Political Theory as open project and appeal

- **We'd like to hear your opinions, points of view, suggestions, criticism... The Fourth Political Theory is not dogmatic** — **it is totally open**. It is just theorising. It is a process open to everybody — to form a theory outside of liberalism and Western political modernity, **with open ends**. Each kind of civilisation, each society, each culture seeks something very special that makes sense only inside of it, not outside.

OTHER BOOKS PUBLISHED BY ARKTOS

Sri Dharma Pravartaka Acharya — *The Dharma Manifesto*

Joakim Andersen — *Rising from the Ruins*

Winston C. Banks — *Excessive Immigration*

Alain de Benoist — *Beyond Human Rights*
Carl Schmitt Today
The Indo-Europeans
Manifesto for a European Renaissance
On the Brink of the Abyss
The Problem of Democracy
Runes and the Origins of Writing
View from the Right (vol. 1–3)

Arthur Moeller van den Bruck — *Germany's Third Empire*

Matt Battaglioli — *The Consequences of Equality*

Kerry Bolton — *The Perversion of Normality*
Revolution from Above
Yockey: A Fascist Odyssey

Isac Boman — *Money Power*

Ricardo Duchesne — *Faustian Man in a Multicultural Age*

Alexander Dugin — *Ethnos and Society*
Ethnosociology
Eurasian Mission
The Fourth Political Theory
Last War of the World-Island
Political Platonism
Putin vs Putin
The Rise of the Fourth Political Theory
The Theory of a Multipolar World

Edward Dutton — *Race Differences in Ethnocentrism*

Mark Dyal — *Hated and Proud*

Clare Ellis — *The Blackening of Europe*

Koenraad Elst — *Return of the Swastika*

Julius Evola — *The Bow and the Club*
Fascism Viewed from the Right
A Handbook for Right-Wing Youth
Metaphysics of Power
Metaphysics of War
The Myth of the Blood
Notes on the Third Reich
The Path of Cinnabar

OTHER BOOKS PUBLISHED BY ARKTOS

OTHER BOOKS PUBLISHED BY ARKTOS

OTHER BOOKS PUBLISHED BY ARKTOS

ce UK Ltd.
K
090123
00006B/522